AF226396

Reinventing Joy

Finding Happiness, Wellness and Meaning in the Second Half of Life

Dr Joy Lim

First published by Ultimate World Publishing 2025
Copyright © 2025 Joy Lim

ISBN

Paperback: 978-1-923583-06-1
Ebook: 978-1-923583-07-8

Joy Lim has asserted her rights under the Copyright, Designs and Patents Act 1988 to be identified as the author of this work. The information in this book is based on the author's experiences and opinions. The publisher specifically disclaims responsibility for any adverse consequences which may result from use of the information contained herein. Permission to use information has been sought by the author. Any breaches will be rectified in further editions of the book.

All rights reserved. No part of this publication may be reproduced, stored in or introduced into a retrieval system, or transmitted in any form, or by any means (electronic, mechanical, photocopying, recording or otherwise) without the prior written permission of the author. Any person who does any unauthorised act in relation to this publication may be liable to criminal prosecution and civil claims for damages. Enquiries should be made through the publisher.

Cover design: Ultimate World Publishing
Layout and typesetting: Ultimate World Publishing
Editor: Marnae Kelley

Ultimate World Publishing
Diamond Creek,
Victoria Australia 3089
www.writeabook.com.au

Dedication

I dedicate this book to my husband, Tomas, the wind beneath my wings, for his unwavering support in all my endeavours;

To my children, Kaye, Renzo, Marcel and Gabby who are my source of inspiration;

And to my mother, Mama Luz, my greatest influence in life.

Contents

Introduction

What is a good life?

I'm so glad you've picked up this book. If you're anything like the many women I've met over the years, you may find yourself grappling with questions that often arise during life's next chapter. What new challenges are around the corner? What else is there to life? How do we cope with the heartaches that come our way? Have we lost our zest, lost people we love or even lost ourselves? Maybe your health has taken a turn, and you're navigating an unexpected and overwhelming health crisis.

Whatever brought you here, my hope is that through this book, you'll begin to uncover the clarity and direction you need to move forward. "A good life" means something different to everyone. But one thing I've come to believe deeply is this: It *is* possible. We just have to choose it and take the steps, however small, to move toward it.

As a GP for more than 40 years, I've walked alongside many women over 60 who feel disconnected and uncertain about what comes next. When the kids move out, careers wind down and friendships shift or fade, it's easy to feel adrift. Some women find themselves caring for aging parents or an unwell partner. Others are faced with grief and the lonely task of rebuilding after loss. In the process, self-care often falls by the wayside, replaced by burnout, frustration and isolation. None of this supports our well-being.

And then, of course, there's the body, our trusted vehicle that, with age, starts to show signs of wear. The choices we've made over decades begin to show up in our health, whether for better or worse. Good health is the foundation of a joyful life, yet not all of us have been blessed with it, whether due to lifestyle, circumstance or genetics. Still, the question remains: What *can* we change? Is it too late to turn things around? Do we really need a wake-up call to take action? And what if we feel we've already done too much damage?

Here's the truth: We all have to start somewhere, and now is as good a time as any. The fact that you've picked up this book and are open to reflection and change is a powerful first step.

We all want happiness. We all want to feel that we matter, to live with meaning, to feel connected and alive. But how do we find that when life keeps shifting under our feet? It's tempting to retreat, to shrink our world or to grow bitter and resigned. But deep down, we know that path only leads to more disconnection. As human beings, we are wired for connection. It's what fuels us.

This book explores the challenges so many of us face and offers a pathway to reconnect with what truly matters. The journey may feel daunting, or it may feel surprisingly simple once we understand what's essential. But it *will* take your commitment and courage.

After decades of treating illness, I now choose to focus on promoting wellness. As we entered retirement, my husband and I have decided on our mantra for living in the coming years. 'Healthy, wealthy and happy till ninety' was what we came up with. While no one knows exactly when we fall off the perch, it helps to have a roadmap. The chapters in this book echo these three concepts. Through these pages, I hope you find not just insight but inspiration to keep going, to keep growing and to rediscover your good life.

Let's walk this path together.

PART 1

Healthy

'The greatest wealth is health.' – Virgil

Chapter 1

Health,
the Greatest Wealth

'The groundwork for all happiness is good health.'
– Leigh Hunt

Food.

Why is it important to talk about food?

Good health starts here as nutrition determines, to a great extent, how we thrive, how we age and eventually how we die.

As we age, food takes on a slightly different importance to our health. While we once needed good food to grow, now we need it more to continue to thrive. Thriving in mature age has a lot to do with not only physical fitness but, more importantly, cognitive fitness.

What kinds of foods are needed to nourish an aging body and mind?

Food is what we put inside our bodies to strengthen it, or on the other hand, cause disease. It is the single biggest tool we have to attaining health. It is of paramount importance that we understand what we can do to optimize the use of this powerful means to health.

Why do we love food? Our ancestors ate food for survival. Thousands of years on, the homo sapiens has evolved its relationship with food. Today we eat not only for survival but have developed new reasons to do so. We eat more when we're stressed, when bored, when idle, like watching TV, or just when we're in the vicinity of food. We eat even when we're not hungry. Moreover, advancement in food processing technology has enabled us to modify (process) our foods not only to serve our need for survival but to serve different interests, like business profit. Initially, processing was done to preserve food to make it last longer, like canning fruits and vegetables in season or curing meat. Later came the ultra-processed foods. Ultra-processed foods are industrial formulations made mostly or entirely from substances derived from foods and additives, which often bear little resemblance to their original forms. It was found that if they combined three essential flavors of sweet, salt and fatty and added crunch to it, this hit the pleasure center of our brains, making us want more and more of it. The resulting product became instantly more popular and propped up sales significantly.

I remember eating my first of these ultra-processed foods when I was in high school in the late 1970s in the Philippines. It was called Chippy. It was one of those crunchy chips and tasted like something I had never tasted before. It was so addicting that I dreamt of the day when I would have a lot of money to afford to eat all the Chippy I wanted.

Over the decades, more and more ultra-processed foods hit the supermarkets and anywhere else food is sold. They have evolved to include food look-alikes, sugary drinks, packaged snacks, instant noodles and reconstituted meat products. Our generation and those that followed became more and more accepting of their availability, palatability and affordability, and they eventually became staples in most diets. Marketing has played a big role in increasing their popularity. The unwary consumer did not stand a chance. Enter obesity, chronic disease, cancers and other modern-day illnesses. The way we now eat has even affected our mental health.

What is our chance of winning this battle to claim back our birthright to health? Where do we even begin? The challenge of changing lifelong habits of unhealthy dietary choices is massive. By the time we hit 60, we would have amassed a lifelong of eating habits, healthy or otherwise. If you are already eating healthy and making all the right food choices, you may skip this chapter. For the rest, please read on and learn with me.

The Gut Microbiome and Fiber

Our intestines and carpeted by trillions of organisms that play a big role in our metabolism. They are called the gut microbiome, a healthy mix of bacteria, viruses and fungi. The fiber in our diet not only helps us stay regular but plays a crucial role in promoting a healthy gut microbiome by serving as a prebiotic, feeding beneficial bacteria and supporting our gut health. Microbes break down fiber to produce chemicals that communicate with our body's immune cells and contribute to a healthy metabolism.

In addition, there are cells in the lining of our gut (called enterochromaffin cells) that, together with the gut microbiome, produce the happy hormone serotonin. In short, our gut microbiome plays a major role not only in digestion but also in shaping the status of our immune system and even our mental health.

Studies have also shown that 'getting enough fiber reduces inflammation and risk for heart disease, stroke, hypertension, obesity, type 2 diabetes, and several cancers, including colon and breast cancer' (Brock, 2024).

Fiber can only come from plants. Thus, it is crucial that we have enough fiber in our daily diets. To comply with our fiber requirements, Australian dietary guidelines recommend eating at least five serves of vegetables a day (one serve = 1 cup raw or ½ cup cooked). Eating the rainbow means eating different colored vegetables to get as varied nutrients as possible, like purple eggplants, orange carrots, yellow pumpkins, red capsicum and green broccoli. Remember when our mothers told us to 'Eat your vegetables, honey'? They were spot on.

When shopping for groceries, it is important to be vigilant. Anything that comes in a box (usually attractively packaged) and has a list of ingredients is more likely processed. It is wiser to veer more towards the fresh food section (no ingredient list) than the middle aisles when shopping. Healthy diets start at the supermarket.

Power of Protein

Protein is needed by our body to build muscles as well as produce hormones and for a well-functioning immune system. This need is more pronounced as we age, the reason why we need to make sure we have enough protein in our diets as we get older. Adults need between 45-80 g of protein a day. It is good to be aware of other nutrients that go with our protein sources. Dr Dean Sherzai and Dr Ayesha Sherzai, co-directors of the Brain Health and Alzheimer's Prevention program at Loma Linda University in the US, explain that 'while proteins can be sourced from plants or meat products, the truth about diets high in meat is that they unequivocally contribute to cognitive decline' (Sherzai, 2017). A steak, for example, is packed with animal fats as well as protein, while lentils have less than 5% fat and have bonus fiber, vitamins and minerals.

Animal sources of protein contain inflammatory saturated fats that result in vascular and cellular damage. This is worsened when eating processed meats like bacon, ham and sausages as these contain flavorings, preservatives and other harmful additives. It is always healthier to steer away from processed foods. Whole food, plant-based diets win the day.

Is it too late to change our lifelong unhealthy eating habits? Not at all. Changing our eating habits to better support healthy aging is possible. I have seen some of my patients reverse disease while doing it.

Elias was a patient of mine who came and told me one day he wanted a referral to a surgeon. He wanted to have gastric sleeve surgery to get rid of the fat that he wasn't able to shift no matter what he did. His cousin did it, and he wanted one for himself as well. He had set his mind to it and planned to access his retirement savings to fund it. He was diabetic and obese. I persuaded him after lengthy counselling to try to do it with lifestyle change first. Thankfully, he was open to it and was very cooperative with the plan I suggested. He was willing to put his decision to get weight loss surgery on hold. Every visit, he comes in smiling, reporting to me that he has started eating better and going to the gym like we planned. His weight hadn't shifted much yet. I continued to encourage him and monitor his blood levels and his other health parameters. After over a year, he was able to get off his metformin (a diabetes medication). His Hemoglobin A1C (the average blood sugar in a period of three months) has consistently been normal for a year without metformin. He stayed on his new lifestyle. He lost weight enough for him to be happy to stay on his current new path and not subject himself to surgery. He was back for follow-up just last week as I write this book, and his A1C continued to be normal. He was a happy chappy, excited to tell his wife that he has reversed his diabetes and lost weight. His *why* was compelling enough that he followed through long enough to achieve his goal.

Success stories like these are not always the norm. A lot depends on the patient's motivation, mindset and perseverance to make the change. There is no one diet that fits all. Our bodies are wired differently, and we work with what our bodies tell us. It is advised to work with a trusted health professional to get guidance and support. But this we know: Changing to a healthier diet is doable for anyone at any age, if we put our minds to it.

-0-0-0-0-0-

Exercise, the Most Powerful Drug for Longevity

When we were younger, we exercised to slim down, to have a nice body or to look good in our clothes. Now we do so for longevity, to prevent dementia, prevent falls, get better sleep, help manage diabetes or hypertension or keep cancers at bay. Those of us with these medical conditions should know well the proven role exercise plays in recovery and disease management. We want to be able to carry those groceries, climb stairs without getting short of breath, do gardening without groaning or squat on the floor to play with grandkids. Our 'whys' have now shifted, and they are now a matter of survival.

Dr Peter Attia, in his profoundly insightful book *Outlive* (Attia, 2023) states that 'study after study has found that regular exercisers live as much as a decade longer than sedentary people. The benefits of exercise begin with any amount of activity north of zero—even brisk walking. High aerobic fitness and strength are associated with longer lifespan and healthspan.'

Muscle loss is one of the features of aging. The process begins earlier than you might think. 'Sarcopenia—defined as age-related muscle loss—can begin at around age 35 and occurs at a rate of 1-2 percent a year for the typical person. After age 60, it can accelerate to 3 percent a year. The loss may be mild, moderate, or severe—or muscles can remain in the normal range' (Harvard Health Publishing, 2023). As we lose muscle mass, we lose strength, making it hard to balance properly. Weak muscles hasten the loss of independence, putting everyday activities out of reach—activities such as walking, cleaning, shopping and even dressing. Every day that we don't use our muscles, they get smaller. Sarcopenia affects nearly half of people over 80. While it is a natural part of aging, it can gradually impact our quality of life, increasing our risk for falls, disability and loss of independence, even death.

Frailty is a medical condition now classed as a form of ailment. It happens when older adults gradually lose the body's built-in reserves, making it harder to cope with daily life demands and stressors. This can manifest as weakness, exhaustion, slow gait, poor balance, weight loss, impaired social skills and cognitive impairment. It is that tiny elderly person who walks very slowly, has very little energy and strength and is forgetful. This person falls more readily and, when they do, is more prone to getting a fracture. This is where strength training, resistance exercises and fall-prevention strategies can work for us. These are very doable exercises that, when done with supervision, may reverse the age-related loss of strength, delay health decline and improve the quality of our later years.

Strong, robust and active is what we want our older selves to be. Enjoying our years with fun and vitality for as long as we can. If we want to avoid the pains of frailty, we need to start working on it—now. The US government's physical activity recommendation is to engage in at least 30 minutes of 'moderate intensity' of aerobic activity, five times a week (or 150 minutes in total), supplemented with two days of strength training targeting all muscle groups. Exercise has been proven to have the greatest power to determine how you want to live out the rest of your life. Is it going to be a life of frailty, incapacity and chronic illness or a life full of joy and vitality? You know the answer.

The day I turned 65, I was walking the tracks of Camino de Santiago in Spain with my husband. This was a hike we never dreamt we'd make, but here we were, together with hundreds of pilgrims who were there for various reasons. The first time I learned about it was after watching the movie, *The Way* starring Martin Sheen. This sparked something in me as something that I can do in this lifetime. I broached the idea to my husband. We could just do one leg of 119 km. 'No way,' he said. He opined that we weren't fit enough for the trek. Still the idea didn't leave my head, and I kept on asking him.

He finally relented on condition that we do a three-month training, after which we should find ourselves having the stamina for it or we wouldn't go. We weren't sedentary people, nor were we the athletic types. After three months of almost daily hikes, each increasing in distance, in different weather conditions and carrying our potential 5 kg backpacks, we found that we were able to build up the cardio for the hike. So off we went. The experience gave us a unique experience of pushing ourselves to our limits. Our feet ached like there was no tomorrow, and our bodies felt spent after a day of walking. But we walked through beautiful forests, foggy mountains, quaint villages, horizons of corn, cows and other farm animals grazing in the fields, clear gurgling brooks and more. Under the hot sun and the rain, we walked. We met people from several countries, young and old, each with a story to tell. We enjoyed local food and discovered how the people in rural Spain lived. We rekindled our faith during days of prayer in the old churches and chapels during each rest stop. Most of all, we felt the exuberance of accomplishment. We discovered what we could accomplish with discipline and determination. We learned that our bodies can respond. Exercise is one of the most powerful 'drugs' we can take if we want an enjoyable, productive life.

-0-0-0-0-0-

Sleep, the Best Medicine for Our Brain

'Sleep is that gold chain that ties health and our bodies together.' – Thomas Dekker

Why is sleep that important? Sleep is not merely a shut eye, nor is it a waste of time unproductively snoozing while we could have done something 'more productive'. When we sleep, our brain and body repairs. Our brain is a mass of nerves called neurons. It is interesting to know that not all of our brain is neurons, though. Around 5-10% of the weight of our brain is made up of cells called microglia. It is part of the glymphatic system, the brain's cleansing system, akin to the sewerage system in our streets, draining toxins, unhealthy proteins, microbes and even unhealthy nerve connections. They 'clean up our brain' during sleep. They work better when we eat nutritious food, exercise, not smoke and are rested and stress free, like when we are sleeping. Thus, sufficient restful sleep (seven-to-eight hours) results in improved cognitive and immune function and enhanced cardiovascular health.

I never put much importance to it growing up. When I was working as a medical resident, training in family medicine for three years, we were rostered to go on duty for 36 hours straight. We would go on call for 24 hours but then we still need to work another 8 hours the following day before we could go home. We would squeeze in quick naps in between calls and admissions, if we were lucky.

I remember feeling lightheaded with my mind floating through the day, as I went about making my ward rounds after a sleepless night on duty. Our 24-hour roster went on every three days. I can only imagine the beating I gave my brain then. That is only in hindsight now.

But fast forward to menopause. This was a really challenging time for sleep. I went for over a year managing with only two to three hours of sleep, if any. I still went about reporting to work the following day as expected. It was that year that I was diagnosed with breast cancer. I think my body caught up with me. Not that this was the only risk factor, but I believe it pushed my health to the brink. Only then did I wake up to the reality that I needed to take care of my body and make changes to my lifestyle, including sleep. Now I make it a point to have my fixed bedtime schedule and prioritize having a restful night. My friends are already aware that I don't go for late nights anymore. Well, mostly. There are exceptions, of course. But any activities after 10 pm are now a rarity. Sleep has earned from me the respect it deserved.

In retirement, we often do not have fixed schedules anymore. This includes a sleep schedule. Gone are the alarms and the bedtimes. We feel that we can stay up as late as we like as there is no fixed waking schedule the following day. But we need to remember that waking up and going to bed at consistent times is critical to health. This predictability helps our body adjust to a regular sleep-wake cycle, making it easier to fall asleep and wake up feeling refreshed. Having a sleep schedule helps our body find a natural rhythm and keeps our sleep-wake cycle healthy. This means waking up at the same time each day, even on weekends, and going to bed at a consistent time as well. This regularity helps our body know when to be alert and energized and when to wind down. Some basic tricks to sleeping better include avoiding caffeine and alcohol before bed, creating a relaxing bedtime routine and avoiding screen time and gadgets prior to bed, otherwise called sleep hygiene.

A study led by Dr Séverine Sabia of Inserm and University College London examined how sleep patterns earlier in life may affect the onset of dementia decades later. The researchers examined data from nearly 8,000 people in Britain starting at age 50. Participants were assessed on a wide variety of measures, including being asked on six occasions how many hours they slept a night. Over the course of the study, 521 participants were diagnosed with dementia, at an average age of 77. Analysis of the data showed that *people in their 50s and 60s getting six hours of sleep or less were at greater risk of developing dementia later.* Compared to those getting normal sleep (defined as 7 hours), people getting less rest each night were 30% more likely to be diagnosed with dementia (Sabia, 2021). So, learn to love sleep as it is the best brain booster.

The benefits of sleep go beyond the brain. Its benefits are felt in every organ of our body. One immediately apparent is its effect on our skin. A good night's sleep supports skin cell renewal, promotes collagen production and helps keep our skin's protective barrier, leading to a brighter, more vibrant complexion. Who wouldn't want that? Poor sleep leads to dull skin and hastens the signs of aging. We are very aware of how we look the day after a sleepless night. And yet we spend so much time and money on trying to look younger with injections, potions and lotions and neglect one of the easiest and cheapest ways to do it—sleep!

Adequate restful sleep is vital to strong immunity, efficient response to vaccines and less severe allergic reactions. It is essential to optimal wound healing, helps fight infections and protects against chronic and life-threatening illnesses.

Now we know how vital a good night sleep is to health. There is another detail worth looking into that can derail our objective to be healthy. That is stress. This is an ever-present reality for as long as we live. How can we optimize health in spite of stress? Let us explore this in the next chapter.

Chapter 2

Health Costs of Stress

Who doesn't know stress?

It needs no definition. It is one word spoken almost on a daily basis by a lot of people. But what does it do to us? Aside from the misery it causes, it can make us gain weight, grow older faster, add wrinkles to our faces and even make us die sooner. So why do we allow this to consume us at times? How can we manage it?

Since our caveman days, we have known stress. Back then, the source of stress was the lion who could be out to get us. We needed stress hormones to fuel the muscles to run, or we'd be eaten. Nowadays, the modern man's lion is very much different. In retirement, more commonly it will come from health issues, financial challenges, shifting relationships or even loneliness.

Recognizing Stress

Not all stress is bad. Acute stress in the form of a mild challenge can even be beneficial. It provides our brain and body a chance to exercise our adaptive response in preparation for future challenges. This may be when we are preparing for a difficult conversation with a loved one or preparing for a big trip. Some tension may be needed to prompt us to finish a task or to go out of our comfort zones to move forward in life.

Hormetic stress is when short bursts of stress stimulate a beneficial adaptive response in an organism. In other words, small doses of stressors that would be damaging in larger amounts can actually enhance resilience, stimulate growth, or improve health at lower levels.

Stress becomes 'bad' when it is chronic and unmanaged as it persistently raises the stress hormone cortisol, which destroys tissues. It predisposes one to developing chronic medical conditions or aggravates existing ones. Symptoms of stress may sometimes not be so apparent. We may simply be more irritable, snapping at people, or we start to lose concentration or be forgetful.

The longer we are stressed, it starts to manifest as recurring headaches, uncontrolled asthma, muscle tension and stiffness, irritability, abdominal reflux symptoms, heart palpitations or diarrhea. Poor appetite and poor sleep are common signs of stress. Sometimes the first time we realize we haven't coped well with stress would be when we are suddenly confronted with a health scare. As it impairs our immune systems, stress can lead to cancer, autoimmune diseases or neurodegenerative diseases.

Managing Stress

The way we support mental health is not much different than what we do for our physical health.

Aerobic exercise like walking, running or cycling are especially beneficial as these increase blood flow to the brain and boost happy hormones like serotonin. This is especially beneficial when done outdoors in nature. I am a fan of exercising outdoors compared to indoors, as in the gym, as we get the added benefit of nature therapy—the invigorating effects of fresh air, the wind on our face, soft sun on our skin, the sounds of birds and soft rustle of the trees swaying in the wind. Nature is the purest pathway to inner peace, and it recharges one's energy and renovates the personality. Studies have shown the healing effects of nature on mental health (Richard-Hamilton, 2021).

Meditation stimulates our parasympathetic nervous system, responsible for 'rest and repair'. If done regularly for 20 minutes twice daily, it calms the mind and boosts creativity. Bob Roth writes in his book, *Strength in Stillness*, 'Transcendental meditation has been shown in more than four hundred scientific studies to show wide ranging benefits for improving brain and cognitive functioning, cardiovascular health and emotional well-being' (Roth, 2018).

Yoga, another form of exercise, involves mental and physical relaxation that may be used to manage stress. Done regularly, this has proven physical and mental benefits. 'When you do yoga, your brain cells develop new connections, and changes occur in brain structure as well as function, resulting in improved cognitive skills such as learning and memory. Yoga strengthens parts of the brain that play a key role in memory, attention, awareness, thought, and language. Think of it as weightlifting for the brain' (Harvard Health Publishing, 2024).

In this day of social media, our constant scrolling, contrary to our belief that we do it to relax, can be a source of stress and anxiety. Limiting screen time helps lower stress levels.

Taking the time to schedule activities with family and friends is another way of managing stress. It can be challenging when people are busy making a living, occupied with everything that demands our time. But making the effort can give so many returns. We have to create our moments. If you open yourself up, it is never too late to make new friends, no matter our stage in life. We can make all the excuses why we can't, but we are only limited by what we tell ourselves we can't do.

Saying No

Sometimes saying *no* is good for our health and can reduce uncalled-for stress. Learning to say no when demands around us do not support our well-being can be a form of self-care. When we say no, we are saying yes to something else. Like our time, our interests or our well-being. Yet, sometimes saying no can be very hard. At any stage in life, situations still arise wherein people and circumstances ask more of us than we can handle.

Saying yes when you really mean no can cause resentment and anger to build up. Over time, this stress eats up inside you and may eventually erode the relationship. It also causes unnecessary internal turmoil, leading to ill health. Knowing when to set your limits is wise because the receiver sometimes doesn't know his or hers. So do not be afraid to say no and allow into your life only those things that you know will support your well-being.

Are we able to delegate? Or just say no?

Gupta, a patient of mine, came to me unhappy. All her married life, she has been the go-to person for family problems. Her adult daughters are not on good terms and not speaking to each other. She is caught in the middle like the net in a tennis match. She lives with her husband, who does not offer to share in addressing the domestic drama. On top of it all, she does all the chores, serving him meals, ironing his clothes, taking him to doctor's appointments. When her husband recently retired, she hoped he would give her more support. But no, he still expected her to carry on as usual, waiting on him like she did in the past. He doesn't go near the kitchen and sits and waits for her to serve his meals. This frustrates her, but she says, 'I can't do anything about it. He has been so used to me serving him'. Thus, her role as the problem-solving, at-your-beck-and-call provider in the family continues. This is a form of silent stress. Repressing frustration can result in illness if not managed well.

Empowered Postures

It is wise to be aware of our body's overt response to stress. A hunched shoulder, a frown or squint, shallow breathing or bowed head can signal that your body is going through negative energy. Did you know that you can physically alter your posture to shift your brain to a more positive emotional state? One way of doing it goes like this: Stand up and straighten your back, move your shoulders backwards, lift your chin up, relax your eyes, eyebrows and forehead. Smile. Focus on holding this posture for a minute and notice how different you feel. It may feel silly, but it works.

Bestselling author Tony Robbins mentioned in one of his live events that we attended in Sydney that one way to manage stress is to 'change your physiology'. Try to do jumping jacks or skip. Smile or laugh, just spontaneously. This tells your brain that you are happy, even if emotionally you may not yet be. Doing this tells your brain you are feeling good because it is getting the happy signal from the body.

Once my husband and I were discussing some stressful topics at length. We saw how drained we felt. My husband suggested we remove ourselves from our environment and go the beach. There, we walked an hour in the fresh outdoors, watching other people, just walking and commenting on how nice the day was. Somehow it made us feel lighter, and we were able to think more clearly when we gave our brains a break.

It's in the Attitude

Retirement can be a time of joyful anticipation and excitement at the sense of freedom and release from the demands of daily grind. However, one can get anxious when suddenly confronted with a lot more free time than they know what to do with. This is especially so once the excitement of things like sleeping in, watching all the shows on TV, playing golf or travelling has waned.

Not having time to do most things can stress us, but having too much time can also lead to unease and boredom. This is what can ail a person who has not taken time to plan what to do with so much time in retirement.

Robert, a patient of mine, used to work as a cleaner at the hospital, a job he enjoyed, before being required to retire. He said he has been working since he was 13, doing all sorts of jobs. This was the first time in his life that he has not worked. This threw him into unfamiliar territory, and he was 'bored to death'. He started to show signs of stress as he did not know what to do with his life. He sits at home all day, watching TV and waiting for his wife, who still works, to come home. He says he is very unhappy and resents that he now has to do the cooking and housework. I suggested he take a hobby or join the Men's Shed in our area, where men get to bond and share skills. A month later when he returned for a script, he was still miserable. I asked him if he had contacted the Men's Shed or started any hobbies, and he answered with a dry smile and said he would get around to it. He was still unhappy with his life.

Rees, a 73-year-old retiree, on the other hand, decided that he would fill his time with all sorts of activities. Talking to him, I could feel his energy. Upon retiring, he decided to drive a small school bus servicing students with disabilities to school. He also teaches young people how to play jumbo drums. He tinkers with his caravan, repairing it as he prepares to travel with it to Tasmania with his wife. He tells me he will go snorkeling and spear fishing there. And to think he is undergoing treatment for chronic leukemia!

Two parallel lives, different health and life circumstances and different outcomes from different attitudes and choices made. One is stressed and the other happy.

We are who we decide to become. If we do not make a conscious life choice, we will float through life aimlessly, like a leaf blown to wherever the wind takes it.

Seeking Help

Some difficult situations can be so pervasive that solutions aren't seen to be forthcoming. Our lives, and those around us, start to be adversely impacted. When this happens, it is very important to know when to seek help. Sometimes our own resources are not enough to manage these life events. It takes courage to seek help. It takes courage to admit our own efforts are not enough.

It is a mark of our love for ourselves and our families to reach out and be willing to be helped. Your own GP can assist you with investigating possible underlying medical conditions, provide counselling, and if needed, refer you to appropriate specialists. Online mental health support resources are also available to assist those who are limited by time or distance.

Medical professionals need the patient's participation in their recovery, and patients are encouraged to put in the effort as much as is doable. Support systems like family, colleagues and friends can be a lifeline. A hobby that uses innate skill does a lot to improve self-esteem. Likewise, shared activities with friends are likely to be more pleasurable.

How we allow stress to affect us is a choice. Victor Frankl, bestselling author of *Man's Search for Meaning,* writes, 'We are never left with nothing as long as we retain the freedom to choose how we will respond' (Frankl, 2006). That freedom is within each one of us. We are free to choose misery or mastery of our emotions and situations. We can choose happiness. Or we can choose to despair. We can choose action or inaction. Our lives will be vastly different depending on the choices we make.

The road to recovery from the effects of stress can be long or short, but I remind myself of this old proverb by Chinese philosopher Lao Tzu every time I face a challenging task: *'The journey of a thousand miles begins with a single step.'*

In the chapter that follows, let's continue to explore how our mind affects our physical health and how we can develop cognitive fitness to achieve the fulfilling lives we all dream about.

Chapter 3

The Beautiful Mind

'You have power over your mind—not outside events. Realize this and you will find strength.'
- Marcus Aurelius

Oftentimes we avoid facing our feelings, fears and emotions as facing them can feel very uncomfortable, even intimidating. Other times, we simply don't want to deal with some of the things we feel. Our days are filled with a lot of noise that crowds out the silence that our minds need. So how do we care for our minds?

Journaling

Journaling helps us identify our emotions and stressors and gain clarity. It can be a way to clear up some mental energy. There are a few steps to doing this. Start writing down everything that's on your mind, literally anything that pops into your head, like the sun by your window or how the roast was cooked last night. Simply put pen on paper. I have only discovered journaling recently and I found that it helped me gain clarity with planning my life, even planning writing this book. You may be surprised at what comes up on paper as you journal your thoughts.

Mental Stimulation

Research has proven that mental stimulation can help keep your brain young by stimulating new nerve connections. Think of it as mental exercise. This includes any 'brainy' activity. Things like puzzles, crosswords or math games can all help boost your memory, concentration and focus skills. My friends and I occasionally play Mahjong, a Chinese four-player board game using tiles, which involves a lot of strategizing and is a nice way to socially connect as well. Reading is a stimulating mental hobby to have. Books enrich our minds in ways beyond the information we derive from it. It can vicariously take us to distant places and make us feel a variety of emotions we least expect to experience.

Exercise

We have earlier discussed how exercise benefits our body. We also know that that it releases those feel-good endorphins that help promote better mood and sleep patterns and reduce stress. Regular aerobic exercise improves memory and cognitive function. Aerobic exercise helps to not only decrease the risk of cognitive decline, but it also lowers dementia risk. All it takes is 30 minutes of moderate-intensity exercise a day, 3-5 days a week. The workouts don't need to be too complicated or intimidating. Think walking, jogging, swimming or even dancing.

Stillness

There is a time for movement and a time to be still. When you have a lot on your mind, being still and silent can be very intimidating. When stressed, we sometimes want to distract ourselves and push stressful thoughts and feelings away as a way to cope. Once we get over that fear and try to be still, it helps us find that peace and clarity.

One of the best ways to embrace stillness and restore that mental balance is through meditation. For beginners, you may find it easy to start with guided meditations. There are meditations apps that can easily be downloaded on your phone. Listening to a teacher just prior to sleeping can be very calming. Yoga is also a form of meditation that helps develop awareness and spiritual strength. For those who are spiritual, time in prayer is very grounding.

Learn

Learning new things and challenging yourself is an important aspect of self-growth. There are countless ways to set small mental challenges daily. I find learning a new recipe very stimulating, fulfilling and exciting even. Even learning a new hobby or rediscovering a talent that has gone into hibernation can help you find confidence and joy in your days.

Digital Detox

Many of us have become attached, even addicted, to our digital tools. How often do you turn off your phone? How many hours of your day is spent scrolling social media and watching how other people live? Constantly checking your phone to see if there are any notifications? How many conversations have been interrupted by this ping?

While digital technology was meant to improve our productivity and save us time, it often does quite the opposite. It is making it very easy for us to waste time. Spending an entire day without your phone, computer or TV might seem impossible, so we may try by doing just a one-hour digital detox. Then slowly you may start to reduce the hours spent on this habit.

Think of some of the things you love doing that don't involve electronics. Try going outside and tinkering in your garden, or read a chapter of the book you've always wanted to read but 'did not have the time', or bake bread. Finding ways to spend some time without electronics may prevent mental stagnation and make your day more interesting.

Cognitive Fitness

What is cognitive fitness? Cognitive fitness not only involves memory but also involves the ability use language effectively and interact with others, control impulses, weigh options and formulate plans. Midlife brings with it the beginning signs of a deteriorating cognition.

Memory lapses can be normal and could be from a variety of causes like tiredness, stress or normal aging. But when one frequently uses the wrong words, struggles to perform tasks like driving (perhaps missing stop signs and red lights), or when one becomes more temperamental and screams at people often, maybe it's time to see the doctor.

Dementia, including Alzheimer's dementia, is one of the most dreaded diseases of our modern world. In Australia alone, statistics in 2023 from the Australian Institute of Health and Welfare showed that it has crept up into the number one leading cause of death in women (Institute of Health and Welfare, Australian Government, 2025). In men, it takes second place. This is staggering! There is such an urgent need for us to do our best to prevent cognitive decline if we are to enjoy what's left of our years.

There are a lot of causes of cognitive decline, and not all are due to dementia. Chronic illnesses like diabetes and heart disease, poor vision and hearing, sleep deprivation or depression can all result in memory impairment. You probably know that diabetes, for example, can lead to complications like kidneys failing or toes needing to be amputated. While we can still thrive with one kidney or without toes, it is hard to thrive when we lose our minds.

How we optimize this ability of our brain to evolve can be the reason why some people achieve a lot and live very fulfilling and creative lives while some have a stagnant existence and wonder why other people are 'just lucky'. Because of neuroplasticity, we can actually *think* our way into realizing our life's dreams.

Mindset

The concept of developing a mindset of visualizing our dreams is nothing new. This has been practiced by people all over the world for years. Napoleon Hill, in his book first published in 1937, *Think and Grow Rich,* said that 'A burning desire to be and to do is the starting point from which the dreamer must take off' (Hill, 1937). His book has thoroughly and vividly explained this concept. Since then, there have been several books, courses and talks and published research about this concept. This is backed by neuroscience.

How can we use this to have the life of our dreams, even in our later years? Is it too late to dream? Absolutely not. There is never a deadline for dreaming. We are limited only by our imagination, and imagining doesn't cost anything.

In 2017 I chanced upon an online course by John Assaraf at Neurogym. It espoused the idea of creating a mindset to support your goals. I followed the course, visualizing and repeating my goals. At that time, our family of seven lived in a four-bedroom home. We had been living there for years, and it was getting crowded as my children grew. We needed a bigger home to accommodate our growing family. We had tried looking for suitable homes for months but could not find one. Following the Neurogym exercises on mind setting, I wrote down on my notepad the house that I wanted for our family. I described how it will be near the river, near the shops and on a hill, a two-story, white house with two columns and a pool, and I described the feeling of joy as I come out of the front door. I did not know where or how to get this house. We went to check out open homes every weekend. One day as we were about to go home from one of the many home inspections, I noted a sign by the road saying that there was a new estate being opened. We went in to investigate. There were not many options left for that phase. We asked about a corner lot that was marked available. It was 11:30 am, and the agent said someone was coming at 12 o'clock to inspect it. Without seeing where it actually was, we made an offer, and it was accepted. The Universe aligned. In April 2019, we moved to a house that we built on this land. We found that the estate backed onto a nice river with a pontoon. Then a Woolworth shopping centre was built a five-minute walk away. The house sat on an elevation with a small forest on the sides. It had two white columns and a pool. I later realized that this was the house as I visualized it in my notebook two years earlier. Working on my mindset actually made my dream home come true.

A happy family relationship? Fun holidays? Robust health? Enough money to live comfortably? Travel to Norway? Once again, we are only limited by our imagination.

May was a 32-year-old nurse who came to me to have a health check. She was worried she may have cancer on her knee. This had been hurting for a while. And her right hip and back were hurting as well, especially when she was moving. May is mindful of her diet, doesn't smoke and is a very fit-looking, active lady who goes to the gym regularly. Her blood tests and scans all came back normal.

Still, she was worried she may have cancer somewhere. We discussed her health risk factors. In her case it was low, but right now, I told her, her strongest risk factor was her mindset. Worrying and ruminating of a possible illness is bad for our health. What we think can become real, and it does. We can think ourselves into health just as we can focus on illness and eventually get ill.

When we assume a grateful mindset for what is in front of us, we open the floodgates for more blessings. When we persevere and diligently ask for anything we need by repeating our visions and feeling like we already have them, things start to happen. We give thanks for the promise to be delivered, and it is given.

Choose a Positive Attitude

Martin Seligman, in his book *Flourish* (Seligman, 2011), discusses positive health assets such as optimism, exercise, love and friendship. Positive emotion, like positive mindset and optimism, is important. Developing positive emotion builds friendship, love, better physical health and more accomplishments in life.

Verona, another patient, came in almost weekly on a motorized wheelchair as walking was very painful. She had back pains, hip pains, leg pains. Every visit was a tale of woe. One day, I decided not to talk too much about her medications and advised her to change her focus away from her aches and pains and towards what she would want her health to be. We discussed focusing on her health goals rather than her fears. She wanted the pain to go away desperately and yearned to be able to walk unaided. She was ready for change. After that visit, she did not show up for several months. I was wondering what happened to her. One day I saw her name on the computer screen. I got excited and, at the same time, apprehensive. What could have happened to this sick lady? I went out to call her name, and I saw her, standing and walking towards me unaided! My jaw dropped. As we walked together in my room, she hugged me as tears rolled down her cheeks. She gave profuse thanks. She has not been back to see me as she was finally able to fly to Sydney to visit the daughter she had not seen for ages, where previously she could not even dream of being able to get on a plane! Even when almost impossible, things can and do change. I once more witnessed the power of our mind when harnessed to its full potential.

We can will so many things, including our health, that can affect our capability to live happier lives.

Happiness doesn't depend on avoiding setbacks, failures, losses and tragedies. All of us will experience these at some point in our lives. Instead, happiness is connected to our attitude. This means consciously deciding not to dwell on the past or worry about the future. It means staying in the present moment and enjoying our time now.

The way to a joyful life always starts from within. Care from within is what we will talk about next. How do we find time for self-care?

'As a man thinketh, so is he.' – Albert Einstein

Chapter 4

Be Kind, Especially to Yourself

'You yourself, as much as anybody in the entire universe, deserve your love and affection.' – Buddha

Why the need to care for ourselves? To love ourselves even? Women are by nature nurturing, taking on the task of caregiving for their children, spouses and parents. It is not unusual that we find ourselves feeling like we have emptied our vessels and don't have time left for ourselves. 'When do we give ourselves the attention we deserve?'

This was the truth that struck me when I was diagnosed with breast cancer in my mid-50s. It took that event for me to realize that I have not really done much self-care. Self-care needs to be done not only at a certain point in life. It needs to be learned and practiced from a young age. As we go about meeting the challenges and demands of our years, caring for our own health should be taken as a priority, not as an afterthought. We go about making time to visit our friends, to give them support. We make time for our spouses and even our adult children when they need help. We visit our elderly parents and care for them. We volunteer to help the community. What about little ol' me?

What is self-care?

Self-care is something we do to nourish our physical, intellectual, emotional, spiritual and social health. Caring for others is indeed a blessing, but we also need to fill our cups so that they can overflow to others. In the process we achieve inner peace, balance, stability and happiness in life.

What are some self-care things we can do?

Health Maintenance

Physical self-care starts with simply moving our bodies. We have discussed this in Chapter 1, but it is worth repeating it here, for it is foundational to self-care. Our bodies are meant to move. When we are in motion, it improves our mood, give us energy, helps manage our weight, improves self-confidence and mental health and contributes to better sleep.

Feeding our bodies with nutritious foods—everyone knows we should do it, but we don't always practice it. When forking a slice of sugary food into our mouths, would it be ok to stop for a second and ask the question, 'Is this going to support my health?' Knowing our whys make us more mindful of our actions. And when we eat mindfully, we have time to make wiser choices. A 20-minute meal, for instance, is helpful for mindful eating. Take time to chew food well, put the fork down between bites and savour the experience of eating. It is good for digestion, and eating when relaxed supports mental health.

Part of self-care is taking care of our appearance. It is not being vain but about honouring our body, including our hair and skin. This now takes more effort as the signs of aging on our external appearance start to slowly creep in. Doing so improves our self-confidence and shows to the world that we respect ourselves as well as others around us.

Finding Gratification

While there is pleasure in buying a new car or a new dress, this pleasure is momentary and fleeting. Gratification, on the other hand, lies in accomplishing something that involves use of our talent, skill and energy. We take momentary pleasure in eating ice cream or watching TV, for instance. Gratification is more long lasting. Like the sense of accomplishment and satisfaction from completing a marathon, climbing a tall mountain, creating a beautiful painting or learning a new dance step. Spending time with loved ones creates happy memories that get stored in our memory bank, ready to be retrieved at any time in the future and relived over and over again. The memory of those experiences lingers. It gives us more lasting happiness. Activities that gratify give us more meaning and are worth pursuing.

Volunteering can be another gratifying activity. When we share a part of our time, some of our talent, some of our skills, we make the world fuller. We take part in the creation of something beyond ourselves. While you might be quite aware of the various forms of volunteering, like the greeters at the airport or minding the library, giving out newspapers at the hospital, working at a charity shop or coaching kids at football, volunteering need not be something grand. It can be also done quietly on our own terms.

Carol, a patient of mine, checks in on her 89-year-old neighbour who lives alone. She brings him food now and then. This very frail single man has no family. He happens to be my patient too. Once he fell in his garden and Carol was there to call the ambulance. He tells me he is very grateful that someone shows him kindness. This, too, is a form of volunteering.

We can look at sharing a part of ourselves as a form of loving ourselves, for when we care for others, the goodness we give out is returned to us a hundredfold. That's how the Universe works. 'Give, and it will be given to you. A good measure, pressed down, shaken together, and running over, will be poured into your lap. For with the measure you use, it will be measured back to you' (Luke 6:38).

Recognizing Boundaries

Making sure we are respected in our relationships is self-love. Recognizing that we need to allow ourselves to be heard, to be listened to, to have our opinions considered, we show respect to ourselves. Sometimes women find themselves in difficult circumstances, situations when finding peace is challenging and difficult. It is at these times that self-reflection is called for. Does this situation support my well-being? What do I need to do to support my welfare and security? How can I show love for myself? These are difficult questions that need brave answers.

We need to nurture our own space. Space doesn't only mean physical space. It is also emotional space. It is a space for us to step back from any drama that may be going on around us. Learning to say no to being involved unnecessarily in drama is a way to protect this emotional space. We still need to be able to function in the roles we have to play, but to keep a healthy balance, there's a limit that we have to set for ourselves.

At some point in my life, I felt burnt out from giving too much to my businesses. My health suffered. Only then did I realize that I needed to protect my emotional and mental space. Sometimes more is expected as people take on more roles. This is true especially for those who take on lead roles in communities. Or even for those who simply have the heart to serve. It is important to remember that the most important person in the equation is you, for you cannot give what you do not have. As it is said, 'Set your limits when you give because the taker can have no limits.' This is not being selfish. It is a setting of boundaries to support and protect our well-being.

Appreciating Time Alone

While there is every benefit to sharing an activity with someone, we may still find joy in doing activities on our own. There is a place for time to be alone, and our minds need it. It can be a time to think, reflect, introspect or just connect with our surroundings. Walking alone in nature or visiting a museum, for instance, can give us mental clarity and be very mind expanding. Of course, hobbies done in solitude can even be a form of meditation, like painting or needle crafting, especially when we get in the flow. When we are in the flow, time stands still. We forget ourselves, get fully immersed in our work and get immeasurable enriching benefits.

Even travelling alone can have its merits and doesn't have to be lonely. I once met a young French lady while I was island hopping with my family in Palawan in the Philippines. While on our small boat with other groups of people, I was curious to see her enjoying herself when she had no company. I chatted with her and found that she worked at a post office in France and saved up as much as she could so she could travel for six months of the year. She then goes back home, works further months and then travels again. She said that she wanted to do this while she still did not have the responsibility of a family. She found out that people were more willing to talk to her when she travelled alone and found it to be very enjoyable. She has just been to Vietnam and Sri Lanka earlier.

I realized we can indeed enjoy our own company when we travel or engage in any other pursuit by ourselves. We have no control as to when we may be placed in a life situation where we find ourselves without a partner or friends are not available. Sometimes we end up alone when they leave the relationship temporarily or permanently. Even in these circumstances, joy can still be found.

Remaining Childlike

As children, we inherently had that sense of wonder and fascination for the world around us. That's why childhood feels so magical. The small ant crawling on the ground can enchant a child endlessly. Even into mature age, we may still reconnect to that inner child that never leaves us. Doing so fosters imagination and sense of self, reduces anxiety and enhances our creativity, bringing more joy into our lives. We need to remove the need for perfectionism when we want to experience the spontaneity of childhood, allowing ourselves to be fascinated by the simplest of things.

How do we allow ourselves to be fascinated? Some activities that may lead to this may be the following: going for a bike ride, camping, fishing, watching a play or going to a concert, painting, photography or swimming in the river. When we do something new just for the experience, removing the need to be perfect or not to make a mess or make a mistake, it frees us to enjoy the moment no matter the outcome. So what if the cake flopped? Laugh it off. The fun you had in the process was the reward.

Self-care is precisely that. Giving ourselves the chance to be happy. To be free of self-criticism or judgment. To allow ourselves to connect to what nurtures us. To untangle away from negative forces.

When we are constantly mindful of what we put in our days, we can more easily catch ourselves doing things that either pull us away or towards our well-being. I like to ask myself this question each time I am deciding on a task that demands my time: 'Will this support my well-being?'

Health Checks

The story of our lived years eventually manifests on our bodies. We may take every effort to care for our health, eat well and exercise, but time always takes its toll. No one is exempt. The line between health and illness gets thinner the older we get. A way of showing love to ourselves is to be proactive with health checks. Seeing the doctor on a regular basis to check our blood levels, our hearts, our skin and lifestyles and getting preventive health screenings can prevent many ailments or catch one early, leading to better outcomes. Even cognitive decline can be minimized or halted with timely lifestyle interventions. I had forgotten to do this very important part of self-care at some point, having been too preoccupied with life's demands. My health suffered as a result. Now I know better. No one will do this for us.

Moving forward in life involves facing our realities, accepting them and making the most of what gets thrown our way. Counting our blessings—health, the love of families and friends, our safe environments, the clean air that we breathe—there is a lot to be grateful for. Having this view can make us look for what is good rather than what we lack. Our attitudes towards these situations and the measures we take towards our wellness make for a life of joy.

You have to love yourself enough, dear one. No one can make you love yourself. No one can encourage you enough, advise your enough or educate your enough to invest in yourself. You have to love yourself enough to take action. At the end of the day, that is what it's going to take.

As we endeavour to do all the right things for our health, there is one thing that we have no control over: the passing of time. How do we use this finite resource so we that can happily answer the question 'Have I lived a good life?'

PART 2
Wealthy

'Wealth is more than money.' – Unknown

Chapter 5

Rich in Time

*'How did it get so late so soon? It's night before it's
afternoon. December is here before it's June.
My goodness, how time has flown!
How did it get so late so soon?' - Dr Seuss*

When we were young are carefree, life and the time seemed
endless. We chased our dreams, tried to build the lives we
hoped for, maybe found a partner and built a family, had
a career and enjoyed life. Then, before we knew it, youth
had suddenly left like smoke, and 60 is now staring us in
the face and old age is beckoning. Time waits for no one.

Statistics have shown that the average healthy 65-year-
old Australian woman can expect to live about 18 more

years. Wow, that's very soon! How do you want to spend that remaining time?

In our younger, achieving years, accomplishment took centre stage in life. As we advance in years, the focus starts to shift. There is less pressure to compete and compare, and a high quality of life doesn't always involve reaching a goal or acquiring more material things. We now need to focus more on our day-to-day journey and make sure this is where our enjoyment lies.

What really matters when we are at the autumn of life? Is it the size of our retirement fund? The investments we have? How big our house was? How much accolades we had? The importance of these possessions starts to pale as we advance in age. At this stage, what we should endeavour to have is as many experiences and memories as we can with the time that we have. Memories created with friends, our communities and the people we love.

Flow

Time well spent. That's the goal. Some of the most well-spent moments we have are spent on flow. What is it? A state of mind called 'flow' is when people engage in highest levels of enjoyment doing activities wherein time just seems to stand still. When in flow, we engage effortlessly, feel in control of our emotions and, most importantly, we do not focus on the end result. When we are in the flow, we live in the present moment and find more joy in the time at hand.

Flow experiences occur when there's a balance between the challenge of an activity and the skill you have in performing it (Phillips, 2013). It can happen when you are engaging in your hobby, like gardening, baking, painting or even when participating in sport or exercise. Make mental notes about how you feel when pursuing your favourite activities and notice when flow has set in.

I remember feeling the flow when I was painting the image of an old house. We were just having a drive at Mount Tambourine near our home when we passed by this white house. After capturing the beautiful image on my phone, I decided to paint the rustic scene on my sketch pad using a mix of acrylic and water colour. I enjoyed the activity so much I did not realize I had sat there for hours. When I finished painting, I remember feeling so joyful at the experience. That framed painting, which I feel was my best yet, now hangs on our wall reminding me of that moment. When I glance at that painting on my way out of the house, it still brings gladness, and I relive the joy I felt in those hours gone by.

Have you experienced flow? It is a unique uplifting feeling that can definitely add fulfillment to your days.

When we wind down our jobs, we have more time on our hands. Even so, not many of us use this time as well as we should. Considering we have a couple decades left, shouldn't we be using this more wisely than ever? We cannot afford to be bored or aimless. The aim we are talking about is not necessarily something tangible or measurable as in the past. We can aim to connect more, to contribute more, to engage more in positive pursuits that support our well-being.

Sharing Our Skills

There are countless ways we can have these experiences. It is our choice to use the intelligence and skills gained over our lifetime to matter in another person's life. We can use this knowledge to have more fulfilment by mentoring, advising or teaching others in a way that does not necessarily produce monetary rewards or prestige. If it does, that would be the icing on the cake. This would be creating not only value with our time but a chance to serve and pass on our knowledge and skills to people who would then be able to make more contributions long after we we're gone.

We can find multiple ways of adding value to our time, big and small. Some people start an advocacy organisation, a non-profit or even a creative business that they wished they had started earlier, but 'work' got in the way. We can also do small, easily doable things. We can teach a young person play the piano. Helping family with grandkids is time well spent as it keeps the spontaneity of youth alive in us while creating beautiful memories for the young, and of course, respite for the parents. Or it may be simply mentoring someone in any skill you have, like teaching someone how to bake! Nothing is too trivial. When shared with a genuine, honest intention to help, everything has value. It makes your time worthwhile.

Creating Moments

Moments do not simply happen. Sometimes, we need to create them. If we are intentional with how we want our days to feel, we become mindful of where we are putting our energy. This will make us realize where our priorities lie. What part of our day is spent with what we truly love?

I remember as a teenager talking to my grandmother, who we fondly call Lola Levi. I loved talking to her and listening to her stories. She did not judge, nor did she lecture. She simply spoke of the experiences she had in her full, well-lived life. She visits us in the city now and then, and I got the opportunity to be with her when her mind was still sharp and clear. She spoke of the value of hard work. I felt at ease talking with her, including topics like how to find a suitable partner in life (which, as a teenager, occupied my mind a lot). I look back with fondness on these nuggets of time with her. I now realize how precious they were.

If you are blessed with grandchildren in your life, what have you shared with them? These are priceless opportunities to connect that can go like the blink of an eye. The chance is so fleeting. Times with the young and old can be a chance to share a part of ourselves and what wisdom we may have, bearing in mind that oftentimes how we act can be a bigger teacher than what we say.

One day, my husband had an angiogram at the hospital. I sat and waited for him at the waiting room. After a while, I wondered whether they would be finished, so I messaged him. 'How are you doing? Do you feel ok?' He said he felt fine. Good. The results? He was told they were fine. 'So, would you like to go to Brisbane?' Brisbane is the bigger city an hour away from us. He said yes, he felt well enough to go. So off we went. We hopped on a train (on a seniors transport card, it's practically free) then walked a bit around the city. I tried on some dresses (I try to resist the temptation to buy any more clothes these days), then window shopped some more. We found a cozy restaurant by the river that we haven't tried before. We had a very nice relaxing lunch. The food was surprisingly superb, and the weather was mild and sunny. We sat and chatted about nothing in particular while admiring the small boats gliding by. Oftentimes, after trying a new restaurant we rate it on a scale of one to ten according to service, food quality and ambiance. We always have a fun time doing it as we give out a few funny ratings. It was a blissful afternoon altogether. We commented on how beautiful the day had been. These simple, spontaneous moments done on a whim can be surprisingly fun. It makes for an interesting day. Experiences like these don't cost much, but the memories they create are priceless and can last a lifetime. We have to go out of our way to create our moments and learn to savour them.

I remember a conversation I had with a wealthy man who still likes putting in 60-90 hour weeks. One day I asked him, 'If time was not an issue, what is it that you really love to do?' He said he would want to read literature and more books on history as they fascinate him. He also would love to be able to play his guitar again. He loved playing the guitar. His answer surprised me as he did not strike me to be the kind of person who is, well, romantic. So, I queried further, 'If that is what you love to do, why are you not doing it?' He answered, 'One day I will do it.' I asked again, 'Why not do it now? Instead of being happy later, you can be happy now.' He countered, 'I don't have the time.' Sometimes it amazes me how we can give all of our time to our careers and leave nothing for ourselves.

Needless Worry

How do we add quality time to our lives? We add meaning by doing activities that bring us joy and add value to our lives, maintaining bonds with friends and family, having a positive mindset, feeling peace and having deep faith in God. We each have to create our own definition of joy and our own version of a meaningful life.

But navigating the different challenges that come to us in mature age oftentimes bring worry about what could be or might not be. Sometimes it may be regret about past mistakes and failures or guilt about missed opportunities with loved ones. Financial uncertainties, like whether or not our nest egg will last us, worries about failing health, worries about difficult relationships or people leaving, all these and more can make for listless nights. But does worrying add quality to our lives?

What does worry really do for us? Does worry make things better or change an outcome? I often get this question from patients when we are dealing with a potentially serious diagnosis. Not knowing the outcome of test results is very unsettling. They often ask, 'Doctor, should I be worried?' While it may be human nature to have this reflex reaction to a potential threat, doing so has never made a difference in any outcome. Conversely, it makes us sicker.

Tomorrow is not guaranteed. We do not have full control of how events turn out. Surely, we can adopt visualization, goal setting and manifesting for the futures that we yearn for, but still nothing is for certain. Worrying does not serve any purpose but only adds to our misery and anxieties.

The next time you catch yourself worrying, divert your thoughts immediately before they take root in your consciousness and spiral you into more anxiety. Appreciate the good things happening in your life, for no matter your life circumstance, there is always something to be grateful for. The house you live in is not nice enough? Be grateful you have a roof over you your head. Your shoes are very old? Be grateful you have feet to wear them on. When we stop the needless distress, the precious limited time that we have is going to be spent more serenely, calmly and joyfully.

'Can any of you, for all his worrying, add one single cubit to his span of life?' Matthew 6:25

People talk about how to have an epic retirement. For some it means travelling the world, having fun experiences, experiencing novel cultures and places, or for some it can mean staying at home and tending to their pets. How we decide to spend this valuable time is our choice. After all, retirement is not the end; it is a project. We appreciate the value of this time and know that it would be too precious a gift to waste. We would not want to allow it to pass without leaving whatever mark we choose to leave. It definitely goes beyond a fat bank account. After we are done and dusted (no pun intended) with life, what will we have to show for it when we are at the pearly gates?

Time is the great equalizer. Nobody has more than 24 hours in a day. How we live each of those 24 hours, the choices we make daily, will spell the difference between a life of little consequence, a life of constant chasing or a life of meaning.

Chapter 6

Abundant Relationships

*'Count your age by friends, not years, count your life
by smiles, not tears.' – John Lennon*

What defines a relationship?

It's when two or more people agree to connect. We enter
into a relationship because we hope to derive happiness
or fulfillment from it. Be it casual friendship or a deeper
connection, we approach it with that hope in mind. For
us to realize this hope, we need to tend to it like a garden
that needs watering to bloom. That watering may happen
in different ways.

Nurturing relationships involves actions that foster connection, understanding and close bonds. Trust and emotional support strengthen this bond.

Respect is a vital ingredient. This can be shown with respect for personal space, respect for time, respect of one's opinion and respect for the person that he or she is. Respect for the other's time may simply be shown by being punctual in meet ups. It shows that you value the other person's time. Respect for their opinion is shown by actively listening with our ears and our eyes. Listening with our eyes is through keen observation and understanding of body language and taking consideration of what they are not saying with their mouths.

Time spent with people special to us is a huge measure of how much importance you put in this bond. Loyalty is shown by being there for them when they're struggling and standing up for them. Equally important would be celebrating with them when they attain success.

Family relations are not made by choice but by circumstance. We also become family by marriage. But family may also be who you choose to live or associate with like hobby groups, church or professional groups. In these relationships, the same ethics apply.

What if I'm single, widowed, unmarried or separated? What if I don't like my husband or partner? What if my children don't speak to me or don't have time for me? What if I don't have children or grandchildren? These questions are not uncommon. And yet, even in these realities, joy is possible.

Why do we need to tend to our relationships?

"The Harvard Study of Adult Development—tracking the lives of 724 men over almost 80 years-—found that close relationships were the strongest predictor of long-term happiness and health, more than money, fame, social class, IQ, or even genetics' (Harvard Gazette, 2017). Dr Robert Waldinger, fourth director of the study, said the 'surprising finding is that our relationships and how happy we are in our relationships has a powerful influence on our health. People who are more socially connected live happier and longer. People's level of satisfaction with their relationships was a better predictor of physical health than their cholesterol levels' (Waldinger, 2017).

While searching through old photo albums for my daughter's wedding reception, I found images from when my kids were young. Smiles frozen in time. Their laughter, the shrieks on carnival rides, the arms wrapped around my waist—all came flooding back. Memories of a life lived. The joy I felt on those days is still in my heart today. No amount of money I earned in the past has given me this joy that has lasted decades and beyond.

Blue zones are certain regions in the world where people have exceptionally long lives, beyond the age of 100. This is due to a lifestyle combining physical activity, low stress, rich social interactions and a diet of local foods. We note that strong social connections always feature in any studies on healthy lifestyles. Okinawa, Japan is one of the blue zones. Like several places in the modern world, young people in Japan leave their smaller towns and move to bigger cities for better career opportunities. This often leaves the elderly in their communities. Instead of being drawn down by the absence of the younger residents, Okinawans are very socially connected with each other and live healthy lifestyles. Aside from healthy food choices and keeping active, rich social connections has been found to be one of the factors responsible for their longevity.

Our busy, modern way of living has been challenging our relationships in more ways than one. People are more mobile these days, and relocating to another city or even migrating to another country is not unusual. This leads to physical separation and can strain a relationship.

Marriage, careers, distance, health or heartbreak all shape our social circles. But our need of another human to interact with, to have a supportive relationship in order to thrive, never ceases. It is what makes for a fuller life.

Life circumstances evolve, and we have to adapt. Creating new relationships offers a chance for expansion and growth. Find your circle, join travel groups, church groups, hobby circles or sports clubs, attend workshops or volunteer in communities. You may even enrol in a class offering new skills like cooking or learning a new language. In your search for a new friend, *be* that friend—available, open, accepting, non-judging and fun to be with. There is happiness to be had around the corner, waiting to be explored. Life is much better with friends.

Relationship with Yourself

Another relationship worth nurturing is with yourself. Happiness from within is the wellspring for the happiness we create around us.

Ursula, 82, has built a happy, meaningful life in the solitude of her small home surrounded by acres of fruit trees. Once a wild storm battered our city, felled a lot of her trees and caused a lot of damage to her home. Heavy rain and howling winds cut off power, and in the darkness, she feared for her life. In the aftermath, emergency services arrived and helped clear the massive debris. When she came to see me at the clinic, she was still visibly shaken. This was the time she seriously considered moving to an over-50s resort nearby and living in a supported environment. Months later, she was back to get a prescription. This time she was back to her usual confident, happy self and told me she decided to stay.

Some people prefer solitude. When one is content and at peace with oneself, happiness can be found in one's own company.

What brings you joy? What do you want to nurture in yourself? We need to reflect on what we value as those things will act as guideposts for the choices we make to achieve inner joy. Bestselling author Tony Robbins, in his book *Awaken the Giant Within* (Robbins, 2013), suggests that we list our moving-toward values. He says, "create a menu of possibilities with lots of ways to make you feel good." I tried to list my ten values and found that they were:

1. Health and vitality - without health, joy is hard to find
2. Love and warmth - they help us blossom
1. Joy - the emotion of champions
2. Learning and growth - essential to thriving
3. Gratitude - brings more of the good things
4. Spirituality - always honour the Source
5. Creativity - creates happy hormones
6. Fun experiences - the icing on the cake of life
7. Achievement - reward for effort
8. Sharing knowledge - fulfilling
9. Contribution to society - our call
10. Financial independence - no worries about money

Whatever yours may be, when the values that we create are dependent on what we can do rather than dependent on other people's action or inaction, it makes it easy for us to feel good. There will be things we can control and those that are beyond us. Let your values guide your actions. When your life aligns with what you truly care about, happiness follows.

Flourish in Relationships

Stable, nurturing relationships act as a buffer against life's challenges and even cognitive decline. Renowned social neuroscientist from the University of Chicago John Cacioppo (Cacioppo, 2024) presented his research on the profound effects of loneliness. His studies reveal that 'the sense of isolation or social rejection not only impairs our cognitive abilities and willpower but also undermines our immune systems, posing health risks as severe as those of obesity or smoking.' We are inherently social creatures, and positive relationships are crucial for our survival.

Martin Seligman, in his book *Flourish* (Seligman, 2011), explains that '*other people* are the best antidote to the downs of life and the single most reliable up.' Every happy moment we ever experienced in life, one way or another, involved other people.

Remember the time when you laughed out loud, when you welcomed the birth of your first grandchild or when you successfully completed a project. These events involved other people. Positive or negative, relationships strongly influence our well-being.

To enhance our well-being, we need to continually stimulate positive social connections. But they don't just happen. Loving relationships take intentional action. They require consistent presence.

Ask yourself, when was the last time you spoke, truly spoke, with someone you love? When was the last time you touched, hugged or shared kind words with them? When was the last time you helped a stranger? How did it feel? Doing an act of kindness is one simple and sure way of increasing our sense of well-being. Doing so also reduces isolation and cultivates a sense of belonging to a greater community.

Decades ago, in the small town where I grew up in Zamboanga in the Philippines, the son of our farmhand graduated from high school but had no means to proceed to college. He spent his time hanging out with other out-of-school boys his age, doing what young boys do. He sometimes came over to my mother's home to clean the yard and do errands. One day, my mother called him and asked him about his plans for his life. He really did not have any. My mother advised him to try spending time helping out at our local church so he could be with people who would be a positive influence. Our home was right across from the church that my mother attended regularly. He followed her advice. He started frequenting the church, helping with what he could. Later she asked him if he was interested in studying to be a priest. He told her he wanted to, after which my mother offered to sponsor his studies. She continued to encourage and support him until, several years later, the day arrived for his ordination. My mother was so excited to buy him his priestly robes. He was now a full-fledged parish priest. He is currently serving some of the remote towns in our province. I catch videos of him in his social media page doing his ministry, showing him riding his motorcycle, crossing rivers and muddy trails to celebrate mass is some far-flung community. My siblings and I send financial support to his various parish projects now and then, as a way of continuing our mother's apostolic work. When my mother died, he came and visited her wake. He offered prayers, gave his blessings and expressed his deep gratitude for the support my mother had given him. I got teary at his discourse and could feel my mother smile looking down at him when he made his visit. Because of him, many people from remote villages are able to have the spiritual guidance and support that they needed. The life of this man could have ended very differently had it not for the concern extended by one person to another. We are all connected by the same thread, and the good that we show to others is akin to doing it to ourselves.

Investing in relationships does not need much. Just our willingness to share of ourselves, our time and concern to reach out to another human being. Tend to them gently, deliberately and often. Even a simple smile can break the ice and is a way of saying to another that 'I see you. You matter.' The joy that we get out of this simple gesture could open the door to possibilities that could enrich our lives.

We now know that tending to our relationships and creating new ones is a way to happiness. Another aspect that needs tending is intellectual growth. Even in mature age, continuous learning is another way of thriving. Let's delve further into how growing in intelligence can make our lives shine.

Chapter 7

Lifelong Learning

*'Anyone who stops learning is old, whether at
20 or 80. Anyone who keeps learning stays young.
The greatest thing in life is to keep your mind young.'*
– Henry Ford

Why do we still need to learn in mature age?

From the moment we are born, we start learning. The baby's brain is like a sponge absorbing everything around her—the colours, the sounds, the feel of her mother's touch. We continue learning as we later attend school, as well as when we informally learn from our day-to-day life experiences and encounters.

The Aging Brain

The knowledge and skills we currently have are fast becoming obsolete in this rapidly developing world. Rules, laws, information, ways of dealing with societies and more—they are continuously evolving faster than we learn them. Technology, for instance, is sprinting ahead before we can even grasp what is in front of us. Everything from travel to language to ways we shop continually changes. We have a choice to stay on the sidelines and wonder what has happened to the world and be left behind or to hop on the ride and experience the satisfaction that this growth allows.

Studies on our aging brains have shown that we can continue learning throughout our lives. Indeed, we can create whatever new nerve connections we want. We can continue to learn and process new information, even if it may be at a slower rate than when we were younger.

Daily life events are an abundant source of new knowledge. Learning how to better interact with people, how to delay gratification, control our tempers, forgive or work towards a goal is learned as we go through life. Our failures and shortcomings are also an opportunity to grow and mature. Resilience is learned through some of life's adverse experiences.

All of us are always learning, whether we are conscious of it or not. Formal learning involved the long years of school, on-the-job trainings, apprenticeships or short courses. We did these to earn a living. Mature-age learning can also be done through experiential learning. This involves hands-on training and active participation.

Experiential learning can be very powerful for adults because they have the life experience and cognitive ability to reflect, develop new ideas and take positive action. It has its limitation in that it is only useful when the content being taught is content that will be used in a real-world setting (Peterson, 2021). But it is an interesting way to learn. And this time, without the pressure of making a living, we can learn in our own pace, and we can learn just for fun.

Neuroplasticity

When we challenge our brain, it grows. It's called neuroplasticity. It sounds like a big word, but it is a process of brain transformation whereby new nerve connections are created and existing ones are strengthened. It is in our best health interest that we do not stop learning. Learning a new language, learning to how to sew, learning to play the guitar or learning how to propagate orchids. It also includes having new experiences. Like driving in a new traffic route or exploring a new city. That's why travel is so mind expanding. When we are at home everything can be routine—housework, watching TV, preparing for bed—and done on automatic mode. They use old neural connections. But when we travel, the brain goes into learning mode. We have to be alert to get to our destinations, to find that restaurant, to catch our rides. Watching new vistas and immersing in different cultures enriches us. We form new nerve connections, and it makes our minds more alert.

Building cognitive reserves protects us from cognitive decline and the symptoms of conditions like dementia. Our brains, when challenged, build more efficient information processing and better problem solving.

Developing a new habit is another way we challenge our brains. When we decide to eat more vegetables or walk daily, we need to repeatedly perform the task before it becomes a habit. Initially it will be difficult and takes a lot of effort. We can slide back into our old ways. Creating new programming takes time, patience and perseverance. After a few months doing it, we see the progress, and by then it takes less effort to go out for that walk. Our brain's adaptability to change is highly influenced by experience, making it a very important factor in learning.

Brain Jog

I drive to work in a set route. Sometimes when I am early, I like to stimulate my brain a little bit and drive around an alternate, longer route. It would not be as relaxed as my usual route, which doesn't really involve much thinking. But in the alternate route, the speed limits are different, and the terrain is more undulating, so I need to be more alert. But by the end, I have given my brain a bit of a workout and have seen a different view, which is stimulating. Have you tried doing this?

Meeting new people is another opportunity for growth and learning. It also enriches our social connections, so important as one of the basic human needs. We can do this in various ways. Attending a local church, bingo sessions, book clubs or exercise or dance classes is a way to meet people. Travelling is a nice opportunity to meet like-minded people. Volunteering keeps us engaged with causes that are important to us and allows us to mingle and meet new acquaintances.

My cousin, Honey, learned how to host a radio program in her mid-60s. She volunteers in a multicultural radio station delivering Filipino life insights to listeners around the world. I found out that it can be a difficult skill to learn when I visited the studio as a guest commentator to talk on health matters. There were so many buttons to press and so much coordinating that needed to be done. Probably easy when you are 20-something. But for me, observing her juggle when to add in the music, then the ads, then splice the talk in order to fit the whole conversation into the time slot all looked very challenging. She has gotten adept at it, starting as someone with no experience. In her own way, she has contributed to the community and got fulfillment out of delivering the service. We can always learn and make an impact at any stage in life.

Technology

Learning new technology is one area that can be a struggle for the mature learner. One option is to check out the local libraries that often offer computer skills training for free. Nowadays, having enough knowledge in technology can be a lifesaver, especially with increasing risks from scams and similar activities. I still sometimes rely on my son for help with navigating challenging computer tasks. Young people effortlessly breeze through them. Years ago, I remember my then 80-year-old mother struggled with it. We had to patiently teach her how to use the computer as she was so used to the old typewriter. She was a fast typist, but the computer keyboards were different, and the computer functions were totally alien to her. But she tried. With our guidance, she was able to meet new friends through social media. We also taught her how to use mobile phone apps. If she had not learnt this, she wouldn't have had the pleasure of communicating with us during the COVID pandemic when we were separated in different countries and couldn't travel.

Nowadays, learning about the use AI is beckoning us. This is one area of technology that is fast encroaching on our daily lives. How do we adapt? This is another point for thought.

The Artist's Way, a book by Julia Cameron (Cameron, 2020), speaks about seeing new perspectives to hone artistic inclinations. It teaches ways to reconnect to our inner creative selves. Reading it, I began to explore new ways of expressing the artist in me. I started to journal, installed a shelving desk in our bedroom for my creative space, was encouraged to visit museums and art shows and decided to attend a furniture flipping workshop, which introduced me to my new interesting hobby. All these because of reading just this one book. A book can indeed broaden our minds and inspire us create new experiences. How many more exciting things await us if we take the time to read a good book?

Solitude

Learning may also be found in quiet solitude. When doing nothing but introspecting without the noise and disturbance of the outside world, our brain gets its much-needed rest and space for new ideas to flourish. Some of the brightest discoveries, insights and light bulb moments can be achieved through this. Bill Gates of Microsoft regularly goes on his twice-a-year retreat. He calls it 'Think

Week,' his period of reflection, learning and uninterrupted thoughts. It was during one of these weeks that his work led to the launch of Internet Explorer in 1995 (Feintuch, 2013).

Giving our brains this space to create is just as important as actively acquiring new knowledge. I find the first few hours of early morning before anyone is awake to be my best time for creative thinking. When a new idea pops into my head, I quickly write it down as it doesn't always stay there once all the world's noise starts to crowd my thoughts.

In these moments of isolation, our brain is forging new nerve connections, strengthening our skills and ability to process new information. Whether it's writing, creating music or playing the guitar, being alone is often what our brain needs to learn and perform activities well.

Personal Development

Personal development is an area that is constantly evolving and is something that anyone can do at any age. A positive mindset, a new positive habit or reframing our thoughts can be learned. Learning to focus on what's good instead of what could go wrong is possible. This is called positive mindset. There are books and courses you can explore to learn these skills. The rewards can really change the direction of your life. It did mine. It has enriched my mind in countless ways and has been instrumental in changing how I perceive life events and circumstances. While the world continues to unfold as it should, looking at it with a wider understanding can make a significant difference in the quality of our life.

Countries worldwide are starting to struggle with the effects of the shrinking workforce as our population ages. Governments are encouraging mature learners to consider learning new skills that can add fulfillment in their lives and enhance self-confidence with the bonus of earning extra income. In Australia, TAFE (vocational college) and several universities and smaller colleges are now offering various courses designed to entice mature learners to join. Some of them are even free. When we reinvent our skills, we may find that there are new and interesting ways of being productive with our time.

Mature Learning

Where can we start? It's a lot easier when we start with something we're passionate about. What are you curious about? What is it that you have always wanted to do? Is it dancing? Or baking? Learning a new language? It can be anything you set your heart on. The way to learn is as varied as you want—schooling, workshops, even the internet is a good source. That's how a lot of people learn nowadays. That's how I learned to make dumplings and bake bread.

Start small, and commit to it for a set time on a regular basis. It is important that you enjoy it, or even better, are passionate about it. Repetition is the mother of excellence. Remember that it is never too late to learn, and the rewards can be incalculable.

Continuous learning and self-improvement keep our minds alert, makes our lives interesting and fun and gives us opportunities to connect and develop our personalities or even discover a new career. Wouldn't this be exciting to explore?

Chapter 8

Travelling Light

*'It is only with the heart that one can see rightly;
what is essential is invisible to the eye.'
- Antoine de Saint-Exupery,* The Little Prince

Clutter. Stuff. Things that people constantly accumulate throughout a lifetime. Acquiring them surely gave us a momentary kick of pleasure, but do they really serve us in the long term?

Why do we need to travel light on this life journey?

The longer we live, the more possessions we accumulate. When our family of seven migrated to Australia in 2006, we had only one piece of luggage each and some boxes for our possessions. They did not even fill a quarter of the four-bedroom rental home we initially lived in. A couple of years later, we moved to our first home. It took one trip for the big removalist truck to relocate all our household stuff. Fast forward 12 years, and we packed once more to move to our newly built home. It took the big removalist truck three trips. We also used all of our cars and the kid's cars to go back and forth several times to transfer more belongings. I couldn't believe the stuff we accumulated in those years!

'Travel light' is the advice we often get when we go on a long journey. Human nature acts otherwise. Just in case. Just like in travel, in life we are often tempted to gather more in the belief that our things will make life easier or make us happier.

Sometimes we gather just because the next person has the latest items, and we should have them too in order to feel that we belong. This is seen in tech, in fast fashion, home décor items, accessories, appliances, you name it—anything that we perceive could give us an easier life or an 'upgraded' life is in that list.

Take tech gadgets, for instance. We are constantly upgrading our TVs, our phones, our laptops not just because we are attracted to newer ones but because the old ones sometimes just stop being efficient. Companies nowadays have what they call planned obsolescence, whereby a product's lifespan is limited by designing it to be non-durable or less efficient. This nudges us to buy more of the newer versions.

In addition, aggressive marketing is constantly bombarding us, convincing us to want something that we may not even need! Thus, the accumulation wheel keeps turning.

How long do they make us happy? Three years? Three months? Three days? Take a look at the designer bag you bought. Where is it now? Is it sitting somewhere in your closet, wrapped in a dust bag? After a while we take new items for granted. It's just human nature. The novelty wears off in no time.

We may note that the more stuff we have, the more we get attached to having more stuff. This stuff in turn requires more energy and cost to maintain. How is that making our lives easier or simpler? On the contrary, it has made life more complicated.

Try to have a look around your home. In ours for example, we have the karaoke machine, which we use twice a year at best. But we needed to buy a good microphone to go with it, and a good speaker. We thought we had to have it for when we have house parties. Our friend's homes have them, so why not? Then there's the mobile phone. Now I need a compact selfie stick and a remote microphone to use for my vlogs. And oh, I also need earphones so I can listen to music at night and a lanyard to hang my phone while I go for walks. It's the domino effect. Not necessarily in a good way.

Decluttering

I am not a minimalist, but I dislike clutter. You can imagine my discomfort at seeing my sons' rooms. But that's a story for another day. I believe that we are somehow shaped by our environment. If we have a clean, clutter-free and orderly environment, we are able to think clearer, feel more relaxed and function more efficiently. We then have a premium called *space*. Every home needs one. When our environment has space, so do our minds. Space frees us to have room to think and experience peace.

Indoor plants give me joy. Plants are good to have at home as they cleanse the air and are very calming. But we can overdo those too, just like everything else. They, too, take up our time as they need care and attention. For instance, I worry mostly about my plants when we go on holiday, more than I am concerned about our house itself. So, is it still good to have plants? Absolutely. But moderation is still called upon to avoid being tethered by them.

Recently, I decided to declutter my wardrobe. I gave away a lot of clothes and shoes. I decided that those that I haven't worn in a year need to go. They filled my entire bed. I called my friends over and they had a field day fitting into my clothes while I got the pleasure of seeing my clothes get used by someone else. The rest went to the Salvation Army. While I was at it, the linen closet was beckoning, then the pantry. I gave away the food processor that I haven't used for years, jars, trays, wine glasses. The food processor found a new home in my daughter's kitchen. The rest went to the Salvos. Then the drawers. Oh, the drawers. They looked like a salad. Dead batteries and mobile phones, cables, calling cards, keys, receipts. Everyone has one of these. I saw a documentary that even Buckingham Palace had some of these drawers. Amazingly, we accumulate, slowly over the years, thinking 'I will have a use for this someday.' The feeling of letting go of clutter is not just that of having more physical but emotional space. It is liberating.

Fumio Sasaki, in his book *Goodbye Things*, mentions that 'Less isn't lack, it's clarity' (Sasaki, 2017). Abundance is not in the number of things we own but how much space we create for ourselves. We often compare ourselves with our friends or even total strangers and feel inadequate.

How often have we caught ourselves trying to acquire the handbag that the lady we saw on social media was carrying? Would you have bought that bag if you had lived alone on an island with nobody to show it to? Who would care if I was wearing a designer dress or one from Target? The COVID pandemic slowed down people's shopping not only because of the restrictions but because there was nowhere to parade our 'nice stuff'! How often do we buy things not out of need but out of keeping up with what others had? I know I was once a victim of this mentality.

Sometimes we hold on to things for sentimental reasons. I have kept the old blouse my mother gave me. Then the home décor my son gave me from his trip to New Zealand from years ago. I held on to them to remind me of the love I felt receiving them or out of respect to the giver. I decided to let them go. I say thank you for the joy they have given me. It's time for someone else to have this experience. There is a time to let go of emotional anchors to clear space for me to move forward.

Constantly I am tempted to get one more thing for the house. It is a challenge for me as I love to decorate my home. I must have been an interior designer in my other life. Nowadays, I am more mindful and know that beauty can be achieved with less.

Does Money Buy Happiness?

We work hard throughout our lives to provide for our families. But past a certain point, what drives us to work can go beyond that. It is not unusual to see millionaires working long hours, sometimes to the exclusion of time for family or relationships.

Numerous studies have been done over the years looking at money and happiness, comparing levels of wealth and levels of happiness in countries around the world. It has consistently shown that GDP alone does not guarantee a country's life satisfaction.

We have to consider not only how much wealth a person or a nation possesses but how much this wealth has contributed to his or her level of happiness. Studies have shown that in the United States, for instance, life satisfaction has been flat for several years, even though the GDP has tripled.

Unfortunately, we have seen a rise in depression and anxiety levels even as communities have increased their material wealth. We may even see that from simply observing people we know. This points to the fact that, after a certain level of safety wherein basic needs have been met, having more money does not always result in more happiness or life satisfaction.

So, what is enough? The answers vary, as what is enough for a typical suburban housewife is different from what is enough for a person on the Forbes 500 richest list.

My relatives who still live in the Philippines have regular jobs and are not what we call wealthy by first-world standards. We regularly visit our families and as per custom, and we often gather with the whole clan, all 24 grandchildren and us, the 'elders'. The joy seen in these gatherings is palpable. There's always food shared (Filipinos love their food), a lot of singing, dancing, laughter and just simple bonding together. These gathering usually last into the late night until we are hoarse. These occasions do not necessarily cost much, but love and sharing make these moments rich.

Having lived there for most of my young life, I have witnessed poverty in several situations. While I was working at a government hospital, it was not uncommon to see patients with no money to buy even the most basic medicines, let alone afford expensive surgeries (not all costs are covered by the government healthcare). Yet they were still able to smile. They were very grateful for the limited resources the hospital was able to provide, and very seldom did we hear any complaints. Families are often at the patient's bedside attending to the patient's needs. Traits like gratitude, strong family ties and resilience can be had even in the lack of material wealth.

Experiences and Moments vs. Things

That stage in life wherein we are cruising into the approaching horizon, we mostly want to enjoy the fruits of our years of hard work. If we have made the right choices earlier, we will have enough to take us through the years in comfort. Nonetheless, not everyone may have prepared as well and may struggle to find the means to retire comfortably. But 'comfort' is a relative word. Regardless of where we are in the financial spectrum, we learn to manage with what we have. We fit the button into the buttonhole.

Visiting department stores has, in the past, been like contact sport for me. The moment my eyes come in contact with something nice, the tackle starts, and guess who wins? The dress often wins. Or the shoes. In recent years, some sense is prevailing. I now try to assess a potential purchase several times before deciding, going through a longer checklist. Where will this go in my closet? Will I have space for it? Do I already own something similar? How will this go with everything else I own? Is it worth this price? Is this item kind to the environment? Is it made from natural materials like cotton, silk, linen or wool, therefore more biodegradable?

Gift giving is another area where I have learned some lessons. For special occasions, I tell my children to try not to give us things, but if they have to give to try to give gifts of experiences or opportunities to create them. One Christmas my son Renzo gave me a gift of Thai cooking lessons with him. It was one of the most memorable gifts I ever received. We spent a whole day learning how to cook tom yum kum and pad thai. It was not only the delicious food we learned to cook, but more than that, it was the hours I spent with my son, laughing, learning, enjoying ourselves. Priceless.

Material things will always be a part of our lives. They make life more comfortable, enjoyable even. But they are not our lives. Things that really matter are not really things.

Our need to travel light extends not only with our 'stuff' but also some other items that can slow us down in this journey. In the next chapter, we will delve into what else we need to let go.

PART 3

Happy

'Being happy doesn't mean that everything is perfect. It means that you've decided to look beyond the imperfections.'
– Unknown

Chapter 9

Letting Go

'Letting go doesn't mean to get rid of. To let go means to let be. When we let be with compassion, things come and go on their own.' – Jack Kornfield

Letting go can be one of the hardest things to do in life. Whether it's letting go of a person, a dream, a version of ourselves, or something we once believed we couldn't live without—the act itself requires courage, surrender and trust.

There is a lot we instinctively hold on to in life that provide security, fulfillment, even an ego boost. So many of us can be caught in the grind we call work to the point of exclusion of nurturing our relationships or even overlooking self-care. I know. I was in that whirlwind for a while. I decided to let go of a profitable business at 65. The temptation to stay on, to matter in my patients' lives, be relevant, not to mention the financial rewards, caused me to vacillate for months on the decision. I asked myself, 'What is it that I hold important?' While my career was important, I felt that there were other things I can do with my life. I realized that what matters most in life is not even things. There is a time to sow, to harvest and then a time to sell the land. Pass it on to other people for their chance to till the land and nurture it like I did over the many years. It has served me well. In the end, nothing is really ours. Moving on to a different chapter in life will offer new opportunities for growth and fulfillment. To have more time to create memories that can last our lifetime. To find new ways to be a blessing to people around. I decided to let go and reinvent my joy.

Letting go is hard. Letting go of a career can be like losing a part of us. If we have allowed our lives to only revolve around our work, it can be doubly hard. That would be like losing our identity. But then there are those whose work have been a source of angst and stress. So for them it can be liberating to let go. It can mean freedom. Wherever we are in that spectrum, this is still a transition that needs some adjusting. New routines, new challenges. For some, it is not knowing what to do with all the time suddenly available. But surely these are exciting times. We are only limited by our own imagination. We can take on new interests, hobbies, projects. Finally, we are able to spend time with friends who may also now have more time to connect. Or read that book that has been sitting on the shelf waiting for us to pick it up. Or take up yoga and learn to meditate. Have slow days. Whatever it takes to take better care of our health. No more rushing. Have time to breathe. This kind of letting go can be liberating.

-0-0-0-0-0-

Grieve Your Losses

It's different when we let go of someone. Be it losing that person who has passed or losing a loved one due to a failed relationship. The aches can last however long it takes to heal. There is no set time. No right time for every person. We heal at our own pace.

We all experience the loss of loved ones and the loss of our own abilities, but few of us have been taught how to properly grieve and mourn. You can find meaning and support through your church or find solace in spending time alone, walking in the woods, speaking with a trusted friend or writing in a journal. When we allow ourselves to fully experience our emotions, it helps us recover our sense of well-being and joy over time.

How do we deal with loss in a way that still supports us? Caring for our well-being is where we can begin. Awareness we did not do anything to deserve this life that we have. We simply emerged out of our mothers' wombs. We can express gratitude by living it as best as we can, with all its challenges. Yes, even the losses. We express gratitude for the learning, the moments, the smiles, even the tears when we were with them. We keep the memories. But that's what they are, memories. They form part of our being, and we take what good we can take from them to where we need to go next. To continue on our journey. Each experience was there for a reason. To humble us perhaps? To make us more resilient? Perhaps even to make us more trusting in God. Whatever the reason, it may not be apparent to us at the time, but for certain they were part of our ripening. Take the plum. It hangs on to the branch for as long as it needs to, battered by the rain and wind. It holds on. It may get bruised, but with time it is sweeter.

Sometimes in our lives, we are challenged by unmet expectations. It may be from our boss at work, our co-workers, our friends who fail to return our call or our families. Especially our families. There are as many sources as we have life interactions. We have certain expectations of behaviour from people we care about, for instance. I did. One of my sons, at one point, challenged my husband's and my patience. It rocked our otherwise harmonious home environment for a time. My husband had a very difficult time understanding how it could come down to where we were. I learned the hard lesson of acceptance. I told my husband that we just need to let go. We don't stop loving but also allow the forces of time evolve as they should. When we have done all we could and nothing seems to budge, we can start by accepting the situation and letting it be. I never stopped praying and trusting God to heal us. Over time, the wounds healed. But we had to let go first.

-0-0-0-0-0-

Forgiveness

Where does forgiveness fit? How important is it for a happy life? I say vital. We may have all the nice material things, the health, the fun experiences, but if there was a thorn in our hearts from a grudge we hold, someone who we have not forgiven from some hurt inflicted on us, somehow we go through life half full. It may just be a small pricking emotion, or it may be severe enough to cause heart disease, even cancer, or affect our mental health. Hate and anger weaken our immune systems. It lowers our body's defences for healing and repair. It predisposes our bodily systems for a fight or flight mode. And we know that when we are in this state, we have more stress hormones released. Our body goes into inflammation, and disease can easily ensue. When we hold a grudge, it is like clutching hot embers in our hand; we are the ones ending up getting burned. Nelson Mandela said, 'You will achieve more in this world with acts of mercy than you will with retribution.' Forgiveness lowers our stress response. Forgiveness releases us from the prison of negative emotions. When we forgive, we are healed. Even if we do not get reciprocated, our intention to do so already releases the burden we carry. Wealthy is the man who is big enough to forgive.

Gratitude

How often have we been grateful? What have we been grateful for?

The more we give thanks, more good things come our way, and we attract happiness. Neuroscience even has an explanation for it. Gratitude activates our brain regions involved in reward processing. It triggers the release of neurotransmitters like the happy hormones serotonin and dopamine, which enhance mood, reduce stress and promote positive feelings of wellness. It has even been shown to improve cognitive function in areas like focus and decision making. It gives us a sense of calm and connectedness, thus enhancing social bonding. The benefits are well known and endless.

Saying a gratitude prayer as you wake up in the morning is a nice way to start the day, feeling gratitude for the little things like a comforting view by the window, the soft comfy bed and the restful sleep. Sleep can be elusive for a lot of people, especially after menopause, and having a good night's sleep can indeed be a real blessing. The running warm water as you take your morning shower is a luxury not everyone is lucky enough to have. Be grateful for that. In the Philippines, we didn't have hot running water, and after a storm, we may not have running water at all for weeks. And what about the car you drive as you head for work? Aren't we grateful we are driving a car that runs well? The traffic? What can be good about it? We can be grateful that we are safe on the road. It may be a good time to reflect on your day. Or pray for loved ones, as I do. Anything is worth giving thanks for. What did we really do to deserve all the things around us? Have we used gratitude often enough? This does not cost us anything. It only takes a moment in our day. Would we do it to improve our level of happiness?

We can discover the abundance deep within us. We sometimes feel the rough seas of life swallow us, and all we see is dark skies. But knowing that though darkness comes, it goes eventually. You know that not a strand of hair falls off your head without God caring for you. These days, a lot of my hair is falling. But then I see tiny ones sprouting, probably not as fast as they fall, but I give thanks. We never forget to give thanks for what is available to us at all times. Finding this self that we long to be, this gracious, accepting self, this grounds us and gives us reason to be grateful. For gratitude opens up our lives to more that we are grateful about and brings in the graces that we never imagined we were worthy of.

We are grateful for having had the opportunity at a job, however simple or however grand, that allowed us to support ourselves and our families and gave us a sense of fulfilment. It is not everything there is, but we can't deny that it is a big part of our lives. Have we found time to say thanks for this? Sometimes we can be led to believe that it has been through our efforts that we have this career, but everything is a grace. The grace of health to do the job, the grace of skills, the grace of intellect, the grace of hard work and perseverance. Because of grace for all of these, we are able to do what we need to do. It is only right to be grateful. It is such a treasure to be able to be grateful.

Vanity, Oh Vanity

The first time I realized I had real wrinkles was when I was 51. It wasn't just a slight crinkling of skin but deep lines at the corners of my eyes when I smiled for photos. I look at the stages of life as, first, youth (maybe until 30) when we try to learn all we can and gather skills. In the sunrise of life, the promise of a new day excites us. We absorb knowledge, we're curious and we are more adventurous. Then comes middle age, from 30-60, when we are at the peak of careers, health and maybe of relationships. This stage is likened to midday, when the sun may be harsh and strong, but it is also the time when a lot of growth happens. We tend to busy ourselves trying to grab at every opportunity wishing there were more hours in the day. Then there's the third stage from 60 onwards.

Like at dusk when the sun's rays are softer. The glow can be a soft yellow, burnt orange or dusty purple. It paints a gentler picture as it slides behind the horizon. Sunsets vary with each person. In the third wave of our life, we can let go of the constant wanting, of the achieving and having. We can be gentle with ourselves and everyone around us. We can let go of hurts, lower our expectations of people and life events. And learn to savour the now.

My life waves followed this trajectory. Nowadays, the hair is starting to grey, the cheeks get more sunken and the skin thins. Of course, with it comes the aches and pains of the body. I get tired more easily, and sleep seems a bit more elusive now. Do I need to hold on to youth? Of course I dyed my hair. Even dabbled in the odd Botox here and there. I now need to take extra care for my skin where before I took it for granted that it was always smooth and my cheeks full. How long are we able to physically set back the hands of time? I admire people who have allowed the passing of time take its own toll naturally. The celebrity faces we see on media nowadays are mostly reshaped by technology and they often end up looking like a different person. In Korea, the plastic surgery industry is so rife that when I once attended an international cosmetic medicine conference, the speaker showed a slide of some 50 Korean beauty queen aspirants, all of whom had very similar features so that it was hard to tell one from another. When there begins to be an accepted 'template' of what is beautiful, imperfections and unique facial features have become unacceptable, thus the need to be changed. But we were never meant to look exactly the same, like clones of each other. We need to celebrate rather than mask our own distinguishing features as part of our own uniqueness. There is nothing inherently wrong with trying to improve on nature, but knowing where to draw the line can be a challenge.

Queen Elizabeth II is well known for many things. But I'm unsure if people had taken note of her beautiful skin and regal white hair. Of her body that grew to be naturally and beautifully robust as she aged but then shrivelled when she fell into illness. She wore the changes very well and with grace. At every stage in her very public life, she exuded confidence in her old age, naturally. I often wondered what skin care routine she had. This is what growing old gracefully is all about. It takes courage to gladly accept the changes that time writes on our face and bodies.

Careers

The decision to let go is often not easy. Same for our careers. We get so used to the routine, the recognition and the financial rewards that go with it. For some, their identities are tied to who they are at their jobs or positions. Positions that have required a lot of investment in education, skills training and years of climbing the ladder can be especially hard to let go. A friend of mine, a fellow GP, who decided to retire got a panic attack when she had to make this decision. Another one yearned to retire but could not bring himself to do it and said he dreads the effect it will have on his health having known his career as the only thing that he enjoys. I vacillated for a year before deciding to retire, held back by similar reasons. The job gave me so much fulfilment that I wondered why I should let go. I felt like my patients needed me and I could still make a difference in their lives.

A few days before I retired, Susan, a patient of mine for the past 19 years, paid me a visit. She brought with her a large gift pack and a flower arranged in a vase. She struggled to carry them to the clinic as she walked with a limp with a walking stick due to hip pains. The reception staff had to help her. She is on the wait list for hip surgery. She came in to say goodbye and give thanks. She has lived alone since her husband left her 18 years ago to singlehandedly raise her two young children, one with serious mental health issues and another with Down syndrome. I was witness to her struggles and tears through the years, not only for her children but her own health as well. Today she shares that her daughter is doing a lot better and is studying nursing. Her son has been transferred to a share home with full-time carers and is very happy where he is. And she has just been granted a community home support package from the government where she can get help with tasks at home. She was crying as she gave profuse gratitude saying I have been her rock through all those years. I could not help but shed a tear myself and felt a lump in my throat at her words. Never did I realize the significant impact this job had on my patient's lives. I told her that what she said made all the years of my work so very worth it. This was the cherry on top of this career that had already given me so much.

Why would I let go?

Then I asked myself, how do I want to spend the limited time I still have on this earth? In my sunset years, would I want to look back with fondness to the time when I sat behind the desk? Surely these years have been a huge part of my life and filled it with amazing opportunities mixed with a lot of challenges.

After carefully weighing my options, I decided to give that time to myself and my loved ones. Much as I loved my patients, I also loved myself.

Sometimes we like to hold on to our careers for as long as we can, sometimes too long, and we forget that there is a life outside of it. We find that when we let go, we discover a life that gives us a different kind of fulfilment that our jobs have not given us. Sometimes letting go can be an opportunity to experience magical moments just waiting to happen.

Declutter Relationships

Lightening doesn't only involve our material possessions. We also need to do so in our personal relationships. Those that do not support our well-being are best to let go. Especially those that weigh us down and prevent us from becoming who we were meant to be. If we engage with positive, supportive people, we grow with them. More meaningful conversations ensue.

Our relationships can get cluttered if we don't tend to them regularly. Miscommunications, unresolved conflicts and unaired grievances can build up over time and create distance between you and the people you care about. Emotional spring cleaning may be worth looking into if any of the relationships in your life have been weighing you down lately. Letting go of unhelpful baggage may make the journey more enjoyable. Travelling through life with just a carry on will take us to places we want to be more easily and joyfully. Identifying what to take with us requires clear introspection and sometimes hard choices if we are to savour the richness of what this journey has in store.

This travel, of course, is also about having fun. For what is life without it? Things that bring smiles and laughter, wonder and excitement, things that give us a rush or even just the glow of contentment are those that make you want to get up in the morning and go. Where can this stuff be found?

Chapter 10

Exciting Stuff

'You're only here for a short visit. Don't hurry. Don't worry. And be sure to smell the flowers along the way.' - Walter Hagen

Why do we need exciting stuff? Well, who doesn't? After decades of hard work, you have reached your destination (I can almost hear the voice of the GPS lady). Is this really your destination? Well, it's actually just another station stop in the short trip called life, but depending on what we do at this stop, it can be an exciting one. Shouldn't we celebrate?

Often in the building, struggling years, women put on hold their enjoyment to prioritize taking care of the kids, running the household, helping pay the mortgage, school fees and house bills, doing, doing, doing. In this next chapter of life, it is time for being.

Excitement does not necessarily mean bungee jumping or getting on a roller coaster. Epic retirement can mean many things to different people. It is finally having the time to do what you really enjoy and hoped to do in the struggle years. In may be gardening or learning a new hobby. Or indeed jumping off an airplane, if that's your thing (a bit risky in my mind, with our brittle bones, but hey, it's your body!).

I know of a couple who sold their home and all their belongings and travelled the world with a suitcase. They seem to be having the time of their lives. Travel, as we know, keeps us alert and in learning mode, and we are required to be physically fit in order to do so while exploring interesting places and meeting people. It's ticking a few boxes. Living in a suitcase may sound a bit extreme for some, but it is doable. Travel is on many a retiree's bucket list.

Doing exciting stuff means engaging in activity and connecting with people. There are a range of activities that can keep us active, mentally and physically, and involve us in opportunities for socialization and even fulfillment.

In Australia we have retirees, fondly called the Gray Nomads, who circumnavigate the Australian continent on a campervan or motorhome, most in a span of a year. They stop at campsites of various towns and cities and explore these places at their leisure. This takes a bit of skill and experience as driving in the great outback could be challenging. But it is very rewarding for those who take the effort and is on the bucket list of a lot of people.

Close enough to caravaning is road tripping. This is what my husband and I prefer to do as we are not brave enough to drive a caravan. We find road tripping a lot of fun. We pack ourselves into our trusty SUV and head off, stop at towns that interest us, sleep at hotels for a night or two, explore the local shops and museums, eat local food, then head off to the next place of interest. We have walked on beaches, hiked forests, wandered at waterfalls, waded in the rivers and watched fantastic views from up a cliff. We found that there were indeed a lot of interesting places right at our doorstep, and we did not need to travel overseas to experience the beauty of fascinating destinations.

People who are keen to travel and want to cut costs may also participate in home exchange groups. There are many to be found where you offer your home for someone or for a family to stay for a period of time while you also go and live in another person's home at a destination you like. There is no cost involved, but there are rules to follow of course. Home Exchange Australia and People Like Us are just two sites you can research to explore the idea, and maybe you'll enjoy this type of holiday.

Others also do home sitting where you offer to house watch somebody's home while they are away on holiday and you get to stay at a location you like for free and have a holiday there yourself. Some involve pet sitting as well. It is something some people prefer to do as a way of immersing in local culture as you get to stay longer and not worry about the cost of accommodation. There are many sites, like Trusted House Sitters or Happy House Sitters, you can visit to explore this option.

Cruising is another way to enjoy a holiday that a lot of more senior people prefer. You only pack once and you get to visit a few different places. You avoid the hassles of airports and dragging heavy luggage, which can be a pain as one gets older. You get to meet people and enjoy the amenities of the cruise ship and its amazing array of entertainment, and of course, the food.

There is this widow from Fort Lauderdale, Florida, Mama Lee, as she was called by ship crew, who was 86 when she sold her home on a 10-acre piece of land and decided to spend 7 years living in the luxury cruise ship Crystal Serenity. She said it cost her $164,000 per year to do that. That cost included a single occupancy stateroom, full board, including the specialty restaurants, amenities and most of all, the entertainment, especially the dance hosts. She loved dancing, and that was her must-have requirement when she chose this ship. No mortgages, no groceries, no bills to pay. I call that cruising through life!

Even when we previously did not have one, taking on a new hobby is definitely possible at any point in life. Now that time is not a constraint, it is only up to us to find that which gives us joy and excitement. Enjoyable activities range from bird watching to dancing, gardening, furniture restoring, pottery making, reading, singing, hiking, baking and the like. Research has shown that the happiest people are those that engaged in three to four hobbies. The more social activities you choose to participate in, the greater your chances of meeting people and at the same time develop your hidden talents. Doing something just for the enjoyment of the activity is very freeing and rewarding.

Volunteering

While not exactly the exciting stuff you may think of, volunteering gives you a sense of purpose and lets you contribute to a greater good. Studies have shown that 25% of volunteers do so on a regular basis. Try and identify the types of organizations you're interested in and see if they can use your abilities. Options for volunteering may be at libraries where you can help sort books and help with fundraises; aged care homes by visiting residents; churches as readers, organizers or lay ministers; museum by leading tours; animal shelters, feeding and grooming animals; second hand shops like Salvos by manning the counters. These activities definitely provide more excitement and fulfillment than sitting at home watching TV.

The options are as wide as your imagination can take you. A friend of mine, Alice, finds fulfillment in visiting the elderly in their homes. She takes them to the shops or just sits and talks with them without any prompting or monetary consideration. I asked her why she does it, and she says her heart goes out to them as they have nobody to talk to, as no one visits them. Some have terminal illnesses, and you can just imagine going through that alone. I think this is a very admirable way to spend time that may even be more valuable to the giver than the recipient.

Sports Are Exciting

Getting involved in any form of sport has a lot of health benefits, especially as we age. It improves flexibility, builds muscle and strength, boosts the immune system and keeps the heart and lungs healthy.

It may not be the ultra-physical contact sports you may have played when younger, but playing sports is an easy way to meet new people and have fun. Lawn bowls is very popular in Australia as well as golf, tennis and water aerobics. What sports are popular in your area? If you were athletic in your younger years, you may even offer to coach younger people. And no one is stopping you from competing in sports. Gladys Burrill began running in 2004 at the age of 86, finishing multiple marathons and setting the record for the oldest woman to finish a marathon with her final run in 2012. You may not be Gladys, but you may definitely try and push your limits of endurance by training regularly. It is wise to consult an exercise physiologist or professional trainer when engaging in the more extreme limits of sports in mature age to avoid injury.

Joining a gym to improve your fitness goals can keep you fit and help you stay active, even if you're not the sporty type. Participating in exercise classes for seniors is a good way to stay accountable for your fitness goals. My husband and I recently enrolled in a strength training class to build some muscles, improve strength and balance and prevent falls. I see older women in the group who are dead lifting 50 kg weights! While are not intending to achieve that level of strength, getting our rhythm in muscle building is a good enough start for us. There is also a yoga studio near our gym that I am eyeing to join one day. A bonus of being more active is that it will help you get a better sleep at night.

Planning fun dates with your partner is one of the best ways to keep that excitement alive. One lazy Friday afternoon, while I was lying on the couch and my husband was watching TV in the next room, I chanced upon a hot air balloon ad. I called out to him and asked him if was interested. Without hesitation, he said yes.

The following day, we awoke at 4 am to meet with our group. We were a group of about 10. It was still very dark, as it was almost winter as we drove several minutes to our lift off point. From our van, we could see in the distance the foggy horizon with a huge dark figure looming ahead. It was our balloon! I got excited. There were three balloons preparing to take off. We climbed in ours, and after several flashes of flames, our balloon started to lift, and up and away we went. The feeling was exhilarating! Watching the sunrise from up a balloon is indescribable! I remember feeling so joyful I could not stop smiling. The view was magnificent, with the hills, trees and endless fields of meadows with tiny cows and horses grazing below. Time seemed to stand still. Finally, it was time to land our ship. We held on as the captain warned us of a possible bump. Thump, thump, thump, we hit the ground, rolled sideways and landed on our backs with our feet up in the air! What a landing! We all laughed as we extricated our tangled selves from the big basket, but our captain was a bit embarrassed at his poor landing skills. Nevertheless, we thoroughly enjoyed the date that we did not really plan for.

Senior Dating

And what about the single seniors? Single seniors also have a lot to potentially gain by meeting and going on small adventures with potential love interests, if that is your thing. Not that being single is necessarily something you may want to change. A lot of single women seniors are very much content with their life situation and do not desire the complexity of a new relationship. But for those who are keen on finding a special someone to share your life with, you may consider exploring possible ways of meeting potential partners. Famous widowed movie actress Boots Anson Roa in the Philippines found a new love of her life and remarried at 69. She said, 'Ang puso ay hindi tumatanda.' (The heart does not age). Love can bloom at any stage in life. The process of finding a new significant other not only gets you out of the house but can enrich your life with experiences of meeting new people, and you get to practice your dating confidence. Potentially, you may meet that special someone you want to spend the rest of your life with. A long time ago, I enrolled my then 76-year-old mother on an online dating service for seniors. Not that there is an age limit for this sort of thing, we reasoned. She was living with our family in Australia, and we were all very busy with our lives, and she was feeling lonely. We thought it might provide her with something interesting to do. Well, she actually met someone, under our watchful eyes, but the friendship only lasted a short while. But even though it ended, I saw her smiling more often and the sparkle showing again in her eyes in that brief period of time. The excitement and happy memories were worth it. You only regret in life what you failed to do but wished you had done.

All these are exciting things, but not every moment of your retirement needs to be packed with activities. Everyone can do with a little downtime now and then, so don't feel guilty about watching a bit of TV or taking a nap or simply sitting with warm cup of coffee admiring your garden, if that's what you feel like doing.

After all, you've earned this time—if you want to relax and do absolutely nothing, then woman, go for it.

'We do not remember days, we remember moments.'
– Cesare Pavese

Chapter 11

Positive Contribution

'We cannot only live for ourselves. A thousand fibres connect us with our fellowmen.' – Herman Melville

In the past, retirement was often viewed as a time for relaxation, travel and pursuing hobbies. Retirement is now being redefined by many. It's increasingly seen as a new chapter filled with opportunities for connection, contribution and personal growth.

Increasing not only our lifespan but, more importantly, our health span is now the goal. Access to improved healthcare and a desire to avoid isolation are seen as key factors for this shift. Many now seek meaningful ways to stay active, engaged and purposeful. I happen to support this mindset.

After having the opportunity to acquire skills and knowledge through life, it may be prudent to try to redistribute some of this knowledge and insight to people who will benefit by sharing the journey of growth. This is called well-being redistribution. Dr Micheal Steger, pioneering psychologist and researcher, spoke at the World Positive Psychology conference in Brisbane, Australia in 2025, which I attended, and discussed the benefits of regenerative psychology. In simple words, it is sharing the good of yourself to benefit others.

At later life stage, it is understandable that energy and creativity levels drop and even motivation levels slow down. On top of that, health issues start to present themselves. With this combination, it is easier to take the slow path, to lie low, say, 'I can't be bothered' and go through the day on autopilot.

These changes can be a normal part of aging, and the call to contribute becomes a hard one to respond to. Contribution can be a big word. What, me? Contributing? I can hardly manage my day! But as they say, 'How do we eat an elephant?' Answer: 'One bite at a time'. If we look at it in smaller chunks, we realize that there are countless ways we can contribute in small daily gestures.

Keeping a tidy home, sharing happily in chores, gives joy to those you live with. Visiting someone you haven't seen in a while may bring a smile to her face. Little acts done with grace is contribution enough to more goodness in our world.

One way I decided to do that was by writing this book. When I write a book, give a talk, guest at a program or do any activity for a group of people, my mantra has always been, 'If there is just one life out there that can benefit and is better off from reading this book (or hearing this talk), then I have achieved my goal'.

Finding Purpose

Contributing to communities gives fulfilment beyond social connections. As mentioned in Chapter 10, this can take many forms. Advocating and supporting causes that align with what we value is a way we can contribute. This is how we find our purpose.

Crystallised intelligence is what mature individuals possess, a lifelong wealth of knowledge and skills that can be passed on to others. Sugar starts out in liquid form but, with constant heat, crystallises into hard solid. That's akin to knowledge packed and sifted through years of education, practice, learning from mistakes and taking risks that may or may not have ended well. Years of gathering knowledge and honing it now takes its condensed form and is too valuable not to be shared. When we do share what we've learned, it brings fulfillment, it gives new meaning and direction to our otherwise *retired* lives.

Mentoring provides a sense of purpose and satisfaction, helping to develop self-confidence for the younger generation of contributors to society. When deciding to retire, we can start to take stock of talents, abilities and wisdom and try to find avenues where we can contribute. Avenues for this may be through school or civic organizations, or you can organize talks about topics of expertise. Many community centres and libraries offer free programs to the public who could benefit from the knowledge of experienced members.

It's not just about giving back; doing this also keep our minds alert and sharp, keeping us connected while we help build something worthwhile. It creates a win-win situation for everyone.

Those blessed with more material wealth may even start philanthropic work or financially contribute to existing organizations with causes close to their heart. A lot of Filipino overseas workers are doing this without really realizing they are doing philanthropy. A lot of them send money back to the Philippines to put family members through school. Or build homes for their aging parents. Many Filipino careers have been built from the sweat of overseas workers.

When we retire, it doesn't mean an end to our relevance to society. It means we can grow our impact in new and more personal ways, doing things we've always wanted to do but never had the time. Sharing wisdom goes beyond mentoring; it's shaping lives and showing others what's possible.

Living by Example

We have previously discussed active ways to contribute. There are also passive ways we can be an agent for positivity around us. And that is by the way we live our lives. Quietly, without fanfare, a lot of people go about living their lives in the way they think best. Managing challenges as they come, rising from traumatic situations, keeping the boat sailing amidst rough seas. We may read some of their stories or even watch them made into movies. But there are countless others who do so quietly.

A life well lived offers encouragement to people around us. Being a trusted friend, a compassionate leader or a kind parent can be looked upon, even modelled, as a motivation for how a life can be better lived. This too is a form of contribution.

We all have role models in life we look up to for influence. We may have one for parenting, one for entrepreneurship, one for creativity, one for discipline or one for physical fitness. Learning how other people overcome adversity, how they started a business, how they rose from failure, or how they developed a skill can all be motivational.

I found my inspiration in parenting from a chemist I knew. She was always very calm and soft spoken (a trait I struggle with) and was always ready with a kind word to say. Aside from being a busy businesswoman, she was gently supportive and helpful to her children and did not push them too hard. She was able to balance her business demands with her parenting, and her children grew up to be very well grounded, motivated adults. I wanted to emulate her. I don't know if I have succeeded, but having interacted with such a personality gave me some hope to be a better parent. I'm sure she is not even aware of it.

Back in early 1970s, our family logging business was devastated as a result of the civil war in our town. Our family's life was turned upside down, and our parents had to pick up the pieces and had to start another form of livelihood. My mother pulled our family together. She grabbed any opportunity she saw that could be a source of income for our family. She started with selling sea snake skins (abundant around our seaside town) to shoemakers. I was with her when she got on the boat to deliver one shipment to Manila, the capital city. We arrived early in the morning, and before we could get breakfast, we had to transport our boxes of goods by jeepney (the local public transport) to a shoe factory in the distant suburb of Marikina. When we arrived, the huge metal gate of the factory was still closed. The factory was in an industrial area where there were no stores around. We sat on the concrete pavement outside the gates while we waited for them to open. I got hungry, but there was no restaurant to get food. Mother reassured me that it wouldn't be too long. We just drank our water. Eventually she was able to sell all our cargo and got a good price for it. We were happy with our good fortune. This experience taught me the value of hard work, delayed gratification, perseverance, rising up from hardship and entrepreneurship. My mother is my greatest hero.

When we contribute, our actions might go unnoticed, and that's okay. There are eyes looking that we do not see. What is important is to do a deed for the right reasons.

The focus is on the honest intention you put out there, rather than on the accolades you get. When working as part of a team, like a fundraiser or helping in the soup kitchen, we don't worry about who gets the credit but on the good that has been shared to those who need it.

Initiate the Change You Want to See

When we wish things to be done better, often it's not enough to sit on the sidelines and wait for it to happen. If we are passionate about the environment, for instance, we don't just preach to people that they should recycle. You can build a compost bin in the backyard or join friends to pick up rubbish from the beach. If you're passionate about helping the homeless in your area, you could talk to or email a council member to advocate any positive change you hope to see in your community.

One day, while going for our usual walk around a nearby park, I noticed that several of the trees lining the pathways were slowly dying. Each tree seemed to be inflicted with some disease as their leaves turned yellow then brown and started dropping off one after another. Poor trees. I emailed our local council member about it and sent her a photo of the trees. Soon enough, parks personnel came and replaced the dead ones and tended to the dying ones. Now all the trees are green and happy again. Sometimes very little effort is needed to be the change we want to see.

Another person I admire is my cousin Honey, who I mentioned in Chapter 7. She has long retired and is now in her early 70s. In 2007, she relocated from Tasmania to Brisbane with her only daughter. One would think she was in unfamiliar territory, not knowing anyone and was starting her life anew with the move. Only a couple of years later, I learned that she had taken on heading the Filipino organization in Brisbane and led the annual independence day celebrations called Barrio Fiesta, attended by tens of thousands of Filipinos and people from various nationalities. It's a whole-day event in June of each year, showcasing Filipino culture, food and music, and it is a fun day out for everyone. It's a huge task to organize, to say the least. Facilitating funding and coordinating renting the huge park, the program and performers, the volunteers, the parking, the stall holders and the police presence and inviting the city mayor and other community leaders—is not a walk in the park. She has been at the helm doing all these voluntarily for over 10 years now. She had her share of challenges managing this big group of volunteers, but she is still there, making sure the events go on as planned every year. She is now considering handing over the baton to younger leaders. But what a lady! I salute her leadership, determination and patience to put herself out there to make a difference.

How can we be an inspiration to others? Mahatma Gandhi famously said, 'Be the change you want to see.' He did exactly that and ended up transforming a whole country's direction. While we may not do grand things, small actions done sincerely and intentionally are all it takes.

What opportunities do you see around you where you could make a difference? Being curious about what other people and communities need can be a good start.

If you feel like you have a contribution to give, taking small actions is a step in the right direction. How can your life be a blessing to others? The more specific you can be, the more purpose your story will have. You may be a hero waiting to happen, if you aren't already one.

You are the script writer of your life. You can edit it as many times as you like. If your life would be made into a movie, what would you want your story to be?

Chapter 12

Spirituality

*'Just as a candle cannot burn without fire, men
cannot live without a spiritual life.' – Buddha*

Imagine the universe with billions of galaxies. The Milky Way, our galaxy, is one of them. The Milky Way alone contains billions of stars, each having planets orbiting it. Our sun is just one of the stars. In the trillion or more planets, the earth is just one of them. In the earth's continents we find countries, cities, suburbs and the streets where we live.

In this street lives you, the human being, composed of body parts called organs. Each organ is composed of cells. Each cell is made up of parts and each of these parts are made up of atoms. The atom is the fundamental unit of matter in the vast universe. Each atom is made up of particles called electrons, neutrons and protons revolving around each other through energy forces. We are all a collection of atoms, walking around on planet earth, trying to live our lives. Everything we have, our bodies and our possessions, are all atoms that are here today and gone tomorrow.

In the grand scheme of things, physically we are all a mass of energy, a very small dot existing in this huge galaxy.

Why is it important to know this? When we contemplate the vastness of the universe in relation to us, how we are a tiny speck of dust visiting this earth for the best of our 80 or so years, floating in this 13-billion-year-old Milky Way, we get a clearer perspective about our lives.

We marvel at the work it took to create our amazing bodies that function so efficiently without us even lifting a finger. Take our breath. We do not need to consciously breathe but it goes on as long as we live. The Life Force is breathing for us. Our hearts beat and blood flows through our veins through no effort or direction from us. How marvellous! How very precious is man to be gifted with something so magnificent!

Spirituality is to accept that sense of connection to something bigger than ourselves. It is a multifaceted concept inviting us to explore our connection to a Greater Being and the world. That there is a Big Force out there orchestrating this big wide world outside and inside of us. This knowledge and realization should humble us and enrich our understanding of our existence.

What did we do to deserve this? We did not do anything. All we did was come out of our mothers' wombs. Yet we are all very special. Have you ever wondered where you are in the grand scheme of things? What force is guiding all the events of your life?

However you may want to refer to this Greater Being—the Universe, Life, God, it is important that we acknowledge our smallness in relation to this Force. Some may refer to this Greater Being as Yahweh, Jehovah or Allah and various other names or references. I am a Catholic and I call Him God. Having the attitude of reverence to God for all creation and to acknowledge His power to guide our paths makes us more attuned with the direction He wants us to take. This faith is crucial if we are to live a meaningful, purpose driven life.

Elizabeth Scott, Ph.D from the University of San Diego discusses spirituality as something that 'isn't just about religious belief—it's about connecting with something outside of yourself that brings meaning and connection to your life. This can involve following an established religious tradition, but it can also focus on spiritual practices like

breathwork, service to others, and spending time in nature'
(Scott, 2024).

Spiritual Wellness

When we have spiritual wellness, we acknowledge this
greater force and can find comfort and recourse when
we encounter difficulties in life. We learn to accept the
things we cannot change and find the strength to face
our challenges.

Spiritual health is a vital component of happiness.

Some of the benefits of spirituality include buffering the
effects of stress and building a stronger social support
system. People who are very spiritual develop more
resilience in adversity. When dealing with hardship in
people around them they can exhibit more empathy and
compassion. They also experience more joy when things
are going right in their lives by practicing gratitude.

It also gives us deeper connection with life and makes us
learn to live in the present moment. It makes us understand
that everything that happens in our life, good or bad, has
a purpose that helps us become who we were meant to be.

There are different paths to spiritual health, and no one
path is the same for everyone. Ways we can practice

spirituality may be through meditation, prayer and contemplation, through connecting with nature or through connecting with others by engaging in group activities to share spiritual experiences.

Meditation

Meditation is the practice of calming the mind and has been used for thousands of years to achieve mental clarity and a heightened sense of awareness. It does not only benefit our brains but our overall sense of well-being. Widely practiced in the Eastern traditions, meditation in now being practiced worldwide to achieve different aims. In Christianity, prayer, coupled with contemplation to connect with the Divine, can be a form of meditation.

I spoke to a psychologist at a conference who shared the time she had as a student when she was required to practice meditation as part of their course requirement. They were instructed to meditate for 15 minutes a day for three months. There was a questionnaire the students had to complete before and after the exercise. To her surprise, the answers she gave the questionnaire three months later showed a much higher score in terms of concentration, creativity, happiness, compassion, etc. I have learned meditation and have been practicing this as regularly as I can, and it has helped me find serenity, especially in periods of stress.

Meditation can be learned, and it's not rocket science, but once done regularly, the benefits are immense. Whatever method you prefer, carving time in your daily routine can keep you centred and balanced during difficult times. In good times, it makes you more grateful for the blessings you have been given. Meditation can involve non-spiritual practices like breathwork, service to others and spending time in nature.

Spirituality in Nature

The Global Footprint Network (Global Footprint Network, 2024) reports that 'at the rate we are going, we use the earth's resources 1.7 times faster than it can regenerate'. We live by borrowing from future generations of earth dwellers. How much longer can we go on this way? If what we desire is to be happy, we have to start somewhere and start now. We cannot simply rely on big organizations or our government to do everything. We need to start taking action with the many ways we can support our environment. Good or bad, what we do eventually comes back to us. Spirituality and respect for mother nature go hand in hand.

What we do for the human being next to us is like doing it to ourselves. What we do for our planet, we do to ourselves. Every creation has a connection with us. We need to live our lives with that reality in mind. When we conserve our natural resources, we conserve our chances of survival and, in fact, our chances for happiness. Spirituality also involves recognizing the greater milieu in which we exist and are responsible for and acknowledging our combined role in its health and preservation.

Did you know that even the trees in the forest are interconnected? I found this out watching a documentary on trees. Apparently, they communicate underground through their network of roots and a network of fungi called mycorrhizae, sometimes called the 'wood wide web'. Trees provide carbohydrates to the fungus while the fungus enhances the trees' ability to absorb water and nutrients. This system reaches as far as the last tree at the edge of the forest. Trees share resources like nutrition and warn each other of threats like droughts or pests and share information on propagation and defences against disease. The bigger trees share nutrition with the saplings underneath.

Perhaps we humans can learn from the trees and shouldn't be much different in the way we support and care for one another. After all, we are similarly interconnected.

Through spirituality, we can enhance our connection to one another and share not only our material resources but, more importantly, our presence. Not everyone is equally blessed with well-being. Some struggle more than others through more challenging life circumstances. But when we are given a sprinkling of this gift, wouldn't it be right to share this well-being to others, just like the trees in the forest?

Spiritual Life

I know of a lady who has lived a life of deep spirituality. She lived not only for herself but for her family and the community she lived in. Well loved, she was always active in any fund-raising event for worthy causes and does not hesitate to offer her help. She had four daughters, and anytime one of them had to give birth, she was there to give support, wherever they may be, even if they lived half a world away. She was a farmer, tending to her rice fields with the help of farm hands. This was where she was happiest, communing with nature, contemplating, watching the green fields and breathing in the fresh air. In her later years, she was back living in the small town where she grew up, where she continued to share her resources. She was an anchor to her siblings and was always ready to lend a helping hand. To celebrate her birthday, she organized packs of food to be given to children she saw playing on the streets and to all the neighbours. Even when bedridden with illness, she continued to be concerned that visitors had something to eat. A few weeks before she passed, she insisted on walking to church to go to confession, sensing that her end was near. She sought His guidance in everything she did and made connecting to God a habit, to the very end. You would have guessed that this woman was my mother.

The universe is mindbogglingly vast. We need to do what we can to find living in this vastness, in a split moment of eternity, to be meaningful and joyful. If each one simply cared enough to give some drops of happiness to others, wouldn't it be beautiful world?

-0-0-0-0-0-

In summary, the joy that can be had in this life stems from a combination of tending to our bodies to have robust health, constantly engaging our mind through creative pursuits and learning, spending time with people we care about and who care about us, cultivating positive emotions through enjoyable experiences, sharing a part of us to others and, most importantly, connecting with our Greater Being, the Source that binds everything together.

Happiness, after all, is more than a fleeting feeling. It is our birthright. Let's reclaim it.

Afterword

The message of hope is sprinkled in every chapter of this book and is for you to find. May you find the one that resonates with you. Hope is the light that guides our ways, as we continue to evolve well into our later years. It is that which makes us turn towards the light, even on cloudy days.

As a parting shot, I would like to share the following quote from movie actress Tilda Swinton:

‘Age is a funny thing. We live in a world obsessed with timelines – marry by this age, succeed by that age, retire by another. Miss a milestone? Society tells you the moment is gone forever.

But here's the truth: that's a lie.
If your twenties were full of doubts, make your forties wild.
If your forties were consumed by responsibilities, dance through your sixties.
If you didn't burn brightly back then—ignite now.
There's no deadline on joy. No expiration date on reinvention. No "too late for dreams".
So, wear the bold colours. Book the ticket. Learn the language. Start over.
Because late? Is always better than never.'

So c'mon, let's reinvent our joys and live our best life yet!

Acknowledgements

I wish to thank my son, Lorenzo Lim, for his valuable technical assistance;

My patients, some of whose health journeys I have shared in this book, for the inspiration they have provided;

And my husband, Tom, for his encouragement and belief in what I can do.

About the Author

Dr Joy Lim has been a practicing GP in Gold Coast, Australia since 2006. She was one of the founders and the managing director of Brygon Medical Centre, a seven-doctor GP practice, for the past 13 years until her retirement in 2025.

She obtained her medical degree from the Cebu Institute of Medicine in the Philippines in 1983 and had residency training in family medicine from Chong Hua Hospital. She obtained her diploma in dermatology from the Institute of Dermatology in Bangkok, Thailand in 1991.

She is a Fellow of the Royal Australian College of General Practitioners, the Australasian Society of Lifestyle Medicine and the Philippine Academy of Family Physicians. She is a certified life and health coach from the Health Coach Institute (USA).

She is a past chairman of the Family Medicine residency training program and past head of the outpatient department at Vicente Sotto Memorial Medical Centre, a tertiary government hospital in Cebu City, Philippines.

Her first book, *Life of Joy*, is an autobiography sharing her insights and lessons learned from the humble beginnings of her life growing up in a small town in Zamboanga in the Philippines to migrating to Australia with her family.

She is married to Tomas Lim and is a mother of four. She is passionate about personal development and women's wellness. She enjoys painting, reading, gardening and hiking.

She was a guest speaker at the Queensland Filipino Women's Award conference at the Brisbane Convention and Exhibition Centre in 2018. She regularly contributes at Filipino Life, a program at 4EB Digital Radio, a multicultural station based in Brisbane Australia, delving into topics on health and well-being.

Her second book, *Reinventing Joy*, finds her navigating the change women go through in the second half of life, helping them find new ways of experiencing joy in the evolving landscape of life.

Disclaimer

The stories cited in this book are actual experiences, but the names of persons have been changed to protect their privacy.

References

Chapter 1

1. Brock, Sharon, MsEd, MS. What is Fiber and Why Is It Important for the Microbiome? Stanford/ Lifestyle Medicine. April 8, 2024.

2. Sherzai, Dean & Ayesha, M.D. The Alzheimer's Solution, Harper One. 2017.

3. Attia, Peter. Outlive, Harmony Books. 2023.

4. Health and Muscle Loss, Harvard Health Publishing, Feb 14, 2023.

5. Sabia, Severine Dr. Lack of Sleep in Middle Age May Increase Dementia Risk, National Institute of Aging. April 27, 2021.

Chapter 2

1. Richard-Hamilton, Franchell, M.D. The Healing Power of Nature, Psychology Today. November 4, 2021.

2. Roth, Bob. Strength in Stillness, The Power of Transcendental Meditation, Simon and Schuster UK Ltd. 2018.

3. Yoga for Better Mental Health, Harvard Health Publishing.

4. Frankl, Viktor E. Man's Search for Meaning, Beacon Press. 2006.

Chapter 3

1. Australian Government, Institute of Health and Welfare Leading Causes of Death, Australian Government. Updated April 9, 2025.

2. Hill, Napoleon. Think and Grow Rich, Mindpower Press. 1937.

3. Seligman, Martin. Flourish, Nicholas Brealey Publishing. 2011.

Chapter 5

1. Phillips, Edward, MD. Go with the Flow: Engagement and Concentration Are Key, Harvard Health Publishing, Harvard Medical School. July 26, 2013.

Chapter 6

1. https:www.robertwaldinger.com.

2. Waldinger, Robert. Psychiatrist, Massachusetts General Hospital, as interviewed in the Harvard Gazette. April 11, 2017.

3. Robbins, Tony. Awaken the Giant Within, Simon & Schuster Paperbacks Ed. 2013.

4. Cacioppo, John. www.johncacioppo.com blog: Human Nature and the Need for social connection. Updated June 21, 2024.

5. Seligman, Martin. Flourish, Nicholas Brealey Publishing. 2011.

Chapter 7

1. O. Peterson, Deb. Overview and Definition of Experiential Learning, ThoughtCo. May 9, 2019.

2. Cameron, Julia. The Artist's Way: A Spiritual Path to Higher Creativity, Souvenir Press. 1992.

3. Feintuch, Rebecca Muller. Bill Gates Spends Two Weeks Alone in the Forest Each Year. Here's Why, Thrive Global. July 23, 2013.

Chapter 8

1. Sasaki, Fumio. Goodbye, Things: The New Japanese Minimalism, Norton & Co. 2015.

Chapter 12

1. Steger, Michael. The Study of Meaning and the Quality of Life, www.michaelfsteger.com.

2. Scott, Elizabeth, Ph.D. VeryWell Mind. October 2, 2024.

3. Global Footprint Network. https://footprintnetwork.org.

Notes

www.ingramcontent.com/pod-product-compliance
Lightning Source LLC
Chambersburg PA
CBHW022053050726
47591CB00002B/515